TO THE NECK AND RISING

TO THE NECK AND RISING

Richard White

ELM HILL

A Division of
HarperCollins Christian Publishing

www.elmhillbooks.com

To the Neck and Rising

Published in Nashville, Tennessee, by Elm Hill, an imprint of Thomas Nelson. Elm Hill and Thomas Nelson are registered trademarks of HarperCollins Christian Publishing, Inc.

Elm Hill titles may be purchased in bulk for educational, business, fund-raising, or sales promotional use. For information, please e-mail SpecialMarkets@ThomasNelson.com.

Scripture quotations marked AMP are from the Amplified° Bible. Copyright © 1954, 1958, 1962, 1964, 1965, 1987 by The Lockman Foundation. Used by permission. (www.Lockman.org)

Scripture quotations marked NASB are from New American Standard Bible°. Copyright © 1960, 1962, 1963, 1968, 1971, 1972, 1973, 1975, 1977, 1995 by The Lockman Foundation. Used by permission. (www.Lockman.org)

Scripture quotations marked NIV are from the Holy Bible, New International Version°, NIV°. Copyright © 1973, 1978, 1984, 2011 by Biblica, Inc.° Used by permission of Zondervan. All rights reserved worldwide. www.Zondervan.com. The "NIV" and "New International Version" are trademarks registered in the United States Patent and Trademark Office by Biblica, Inc.°

Scripture quotations marked NLT are from the Holy Bible, New Living Translation. © 1996, 2004, 2007, 2013, 2015 by Tyndale House Foundation. Used by permission of Tyndale House Publishers, Inc., Carol Stream, Illinois 60188. All rights reserved.

Scripture quotations marked NKJV are from the New King James Version°. © 1982 by Thomas Nelson. Used by permission. All rights reserved.

Scripture quotations marked THE MESSAGE are from The Message. Copyright © by Eugene H. Peterson 1993, 1994, 1995, 1996, 2000, 2001, 2002. Used by permission of NavPress. All rights reserved. Represented by Tyndale House Publishers, Inc.

Library of Congress Cataloging-in-Publication Data

Library of Congress Control Number: 2019930381

ISBN 978-1-400325313 (Paperback)
ISBN 978-1-400325320 (Hardbound)
ISBN 978-1-400325528 (eBook)

DEDICATION

To my beautiful wife Jenny, who is my best friend, confidante and biggest advocate. She constantly reminds me of my value and has championed a belief in my own sense of worth. In some ways, this book would not have made the light of day if it hadn't been for her encouragement and patience. You are indeed my favourite first wife.

ACKNOWLEDGEMENTS

I need to thank the following people for their availability and willingness to assist me from various perspectives and God-given skills.

Brian Keyte, for his assistance with my English and general all-round encouragement. I feel honoured that you were the first person to have read my manuscript in its entirety.

Rabbi Philip Heilbrunn, BA LLB: former head rabbi, St. Kilda Synagogue, historical and cultural authenticity

The following people for reading my manuscript and providing me with valuable feedback:

Christine Brown, Dave and Bec Owens, Dave Hermann, Lil O'Brien

CONTENTS

INTRODUCTION

The period from the mid 2008 to early 2009 was an extremely difficult and emotional time in my life. There were a number of pressures that were pushing me through what seemed to be a never-ending emotional roller coaster where I had no control. I had experienced this once before but not for the same reasons or, for that matter, to the same depths. Emotionally, I was experiencing an extended period of flatness. I had difficulty sleeping; my mind would be constantly thinking of work. All I wanted to do was sit, mope and watch TV. There were times when I was on the verge of spontaneous tears. I could often feel them building up.

Through this period, I also had responsibilities in the life of the church we attend. I was facilitating a men's course, and yet I had my own emotional baggage to deal with as I was leading this small group of men on their own journey of discovery and healing. Thankfully, I had a co-facilitator who stepped up and was fantastic during this time and assisted me greatly. Thank you, Wayne. You are a champion!

It was during this period of time when one word caught my attention. The word was "broken-hearted." I looked it up in my concordance and one of the passages of scripture it directed me to was Psalm 69.

I looked at the verse about broken-hearted to get some context, and there it was, like a slap to the face:

"Save me O God for the waters are up to my neck"

(PSALM 69:1)

That was what my life was like, described by David so articulately. That metaphor resonated so true—I did feel as though I was drowning. There was no better way to describe how I felt at that time than through that use of that particular metaphor.

We Don't Communicate

Over time, I have discovered there are certain times and situations when men exhibit difficulty in assessing and communicating how they feel. They are either uncertain or cannot clearly articulate their emotions. This can even be to the point of not being able to describe those feelings in simple picture form. Men particularly—I know I am one—do not possess the emotional vocabulary to clearly describe how they feel. Part of my journey over the previous six years had been to identify those very things, to be able to verbalise how I felt. An introvert by nature, I was quite happy to let life ride on by. I was in cruise control. Our children were growing and soon we would be empty nesters, so I needed to reconnect with my wife or our marriage would not last the journey. We had begun this journey of purposefully working on our relationship. We read books, did courses and even facilitated those very same courses. We strategically chose to do whatever it would take to make our marriage work. I needed to confront the challenges, and yet while doing that, I found myself being drowned in a sea of emotion that I could not identify or wanted to acknowledge. The burden I felt while journeying with men and couples, while simultaneously working through my own brokenness, seemed unbearable at times. The lesson I learned through all this was that God is indeed faithful and true to His Word. His work of grace was sufficient to give me the capacity to confront the aspects of my life that He wanted to be addressed. I could not have done this without the support of my beautiful wife. Her love and positive words were a balm to my soul.

Words may not be used but our actions or reactions dictate the terms. Very often, it is not our words that draw the attention of our loved ones, but what is not said that catches their attention. Our vocabulary and phraseology is limited to:

"I'm fine."
"Nothing is the matter."
"Get off my back."

As a result, we lash out; we fight and take undue risks in an effort to disguise our self-perceived weaknesses which, when it is boiled down, are only our inability to communicate adequately or appropriately. We will do whatever it takes to bury those inadequacies and deflect blame where possible. This is a pattern of learned behaviour, either through life's experiences or as a result of poor role modelling by our fathers or from men in general. This may be a generalisation, but I acknowledge there are also men who can describe how they feel and have developed a good emotional vocabulary from which to draw. Whether this is a natural phenomenon or the result of a journey is difficult to determine without undertaking a major interview and research process.

King David, as a poet/songwriter, had the ability to articulate his feelings and describe his emotional mood. At various times throughout the Psalms, David expressed his fears, the high and low points, feelings of alienation, his sense of loneliness and isolation, and remorse when confronted with sin in his life. Not only could David provide an emotional journey, he was able to describe his emotional state. One particular method of description is through the use of metaphor. A metaphor is a powerful tool of description. This can be especially true when describing our emotional state. Our choice of phrase can create a fantastic word picture that can assist in articulating to the listener that, in turn, leads to a point of identification. We can feel that we have been heard, and that our point has been put across. We do not need to provide any further explanation.

The purpose of this book is to draw people's attention to the plight of individuals in our society, who struggle through life under the cloud of depression. In many ways they are silent sufferers. These people are afraid to speak up for fear of either being misunderstood or judged by others. People can be very uncomfortable when they are confronted with someone who is in a state of depression. But truthfully, these are normal human beings who have an illness. It may not be something that is visible like a broken arm or leg but can be just as debilitating to that person. It was only after I had the outline for this book, and my subsequent research, that revealed the similarities that existed between the major points that you will read in the following pages and some of the clinical signs of depression. I knew then that this book was meant to be written.

This book should be viewed as a series of personal reflections based on a passage of Scripture, in this case a Psalm, and should in no way be considered as a textbook or a comprehensive study on depression and its causes. The fact that those similarities exist were unintended. I can only go where my thoughts and the subject material has taken me.

Some chapters have been easier to communicate through the written word, as I have personal experience to draw from, while others have been made more difficult. Those that have been more difficult to write, I have had to rely on the experiences of others to provide me with a point of reference. Thank you to those individuals.

Likewise, as you read the book, there may be areas that you will identify with quite easily, and other's aspects, not so much. Please do not rush through the book; it hasn't been written so you can read it in one sitting. Take your time to be reflective and even devotional in approaching it. Work with your emotions and actively engage with them, as I have done throughout writing this book. Through my journey I have discovered some valuable resources and have included some of the research and academic papers, as I have found their contents helpful to me.

A Personal Journey

I have been on my own journey of discovery. I believe that God has shown me principles that have helped me during that journey. In many ways, this voyage of discovery has helped me understand who I am. I know the absolutes of God, His love for me, how I am valued and that God has a purpose for my life, but at the same time there has been a degree of disconnect from those truths brought about by life's experience that have "separated me" from those truths. This is not to say that I do not believe in those absolutes. I do. They are truth. Absolutes, by definition, cannot change and cannot be changed. Life's experiences do provide the framework for our personal beliefs. Our level of reality is shaped by what we have experienced in our life, but that does not make those beliefs right. When taken to extremes, that concept of reality brought about through experience becomes truth as we know it and, as such, can countermand the absolutes of God and make them seem unattainable in belief and, by default, separate us from the Truth.

Absolutes show us that:

"God is good"—but there are people who suffer bad things.

"God is our healer"—but not everyone is healed.

"God is our provider"—but there are people who experience lack.

As you can see from these examples, our perception of God may become clouded by what we experience, or our perception lends itself to those beliefs but really, at the end of the day, the absolutes still stand. It may be difficult to move our thinking in line with the truths regarding God, but is not impossible. This is where faith in God is integral, because we must bring our thinking into line with God's Word. Romans Chapter 12 tells us that we are to be transformed by the renewal of our minds. This is not just a renewal that needs to occur when we accept Christ, but also at times when our thinking becomes clouded. I am not speaking of positive thinking or living in denial of events that have occurred in our lives. We need to accept that we cannot change events, but we can control the effect those events have on our future. If we hold on to the negative aspects of life's events, we may become bitter, or we will live in perpetual motion, holding on to our hurts. We allow past events to control our present and future. In the end, we choose how those events are viewed and how they control our present-day attitudes and behaviours. Choice is a major component when we talk about inner healing, as we can choose to be either negative or positive.

Events Can Affect Us

If, for example, we have experienced tragedy on several occasions in our life, we may tend to take a more negative view in our outlook. Also, if we have been subject to deception by others, we will become sceptical of others and develop an inability to trust others. Often, we may blame God for our lot, but really, our choices have defined outcomes in our lives. We may ask, "Why did God allow that to happen?" "If He is such a loving God, how come this has happened to me?"

In writing this book, I make no apologies for some of the things I will say or express. This will be very much from this man's perspective; I have no other point of reference. This is a result of my own personal journey. But the Grace of God has also influenced some of my attitudes. Personal experience can be a harsh teacher, especially if we have made poor choices. My desire is to use the word God has placed in my heart and, while it has given me solace in a time of inner turmoil, to also be an encouragement to you, the reader. Initially, the challenge for me was to work with God rather than offer resistance. I had a choice to make; the final decision was mine to make. That is God's way. In some ways, my writing has been personally cathartic, but at the end of the day, I want to see this book help people in their own personal journey. Maybe it will be figuratively a branch that is reached out in rescue for those who are in the waters up to their necks and it is rising.

It is interesting to note that even though Psalm 69 has such poignant content, it is also a widely quoted portion of Old Testament Scripture in the New Testament; it is quoted on twenty-three occasions (cross referenced through *New American Standard Bible*). This is only second to Psalm 22. Jesus is attributed to have quoted from this Psalm eleven times throughout the four gospels. Those quotations were made during the last few days prior to and during his crucifixion.

The text will be studied in a manner that will see us explore the metaphor of the floodwaters as described by David and the aspects of his journey that he highlighted. Through my research, to date, I have been unable to find a work of literature that explores this aspect of emotion as it can be drawn from Psalm 69. I have relied on those who have gone before me for scriptural and theological comments. Their language may be of an age gone by but their message is no less relevant, and we can learn much from these people who persevered through their own challenges of faith and championed the way we view much of what we now understand of our God.

I add to this introduction. July 6, 2013, I received a call from my younger sister. She was distraught; our little brother has been found dead in his room. For a period of time, he had experienced depression caused by a variety of life's road humps. There had been times when I had spoken to him on the phone and you could hear his downcast spirit. From my own sense of fragility, I attempted to encourage his spirit and for him to turn to God as his resource. This was difficult, as he was my only brother, the late-night call with the news and that accompanying sense of loss. I know that I am not or will be the only person to have ever experienced this pain. But, men, and at this point I specifically speak to you. Come down from your towers of isolation and from behind your battlements where you hide yourselves. Through it all, though, I know my Redeemer lives.

CHAPTER 1

THE METAPHOR OF THE
FLOODWATERS

In emotional healing, men particularly possess an inability to clearly articulate where they are at, either in times of crisis or, for that matter, in "normal" everyday life. Men seem to have been conditioned by society that vulnerabilities are a form of weakness and, as a consequence, they bring into question their very masculinity. This mindset robs men of the true liberating freedom that comes with dealing with emotional issues in a healthy manner. The atypical man is often described as the strong, silent type. It is only as you begin to know him that you discover just how strong and silent he really is. Society often views the silence in the male as a source of his strength. It demonstrates that he has everything under control. But this is a persona, a great cover up—a big fat lie. The word "lie" may sound a bit strong, but a lie is a lie is a lie. Let's be true to ourselves and call a spade a spade. It is time to stop dancing around with semantics. Using particular words or language to reduce the impact or as a means of deflection is paramount to giving

1

the lie credibility that it is not due. I feel particularly strongly about this because I have perpetuated my own lie and have learned that it is of no benefit to me or to those around me. Until we recognise and acknowledge this aspect of our psyche, we will continue to perpetuate the lie. If we cannot be true to self, how can we be truthful with others?

David began this Psalm with some direction which, in this case, is for the choir director or chief musician. There is direction for the psalm to be sung to a particular tune: "lilies" or "upon Shoshannim," as translated in the *King James*. My readings on this theme of Shoshannim have been, on the main, incomplete, as there is limited information available as to the exact meaning of the word. The word "lilies" seems to be a word that is associated with Shoshannim, or it is a musical instrument not too dissimilar in shape to a lily. There is also a school of thought in Jewish theology that Shoshannim means *rose* and more directly related to what they see as the key theme of the Psalm as being exile. Given the descriptiveness of the metaphor and how David expressed his anxiety, a rose would be a more appropriate floral companion because of its thorns amid beauty through to the rich red colour and the fragrance of its perfume, as opposed to a lily, where the lines are smooth and defined, with the colours exhibiting a form of purity. We will explore this thought in greater depth in later chapters.

As I have already mentioned, there are also men who have learned this valuable lesson and developed the capabilities to identify their emotions and what is driving a particular feeling at a given time was written. Albert Barnes contended that there are a number of occasions when this might have been applicable, but by "most natural interpretation," as he termed it, places the writing of this Psalm during the rebellion of Absalom. R. A. Torrey *(Treasury of Scripture Knowledge)* made a similar acknowledgement. At that time, there was immense external pressure coming upon David. His son had taken it on himself to avenge the rape of his sister. Absalom, in his anger, had taken on the offence because of his father's apparent inability to act.

Karl Keil (1807–1888) and Friedrich Delitzsch (1813–1890), noted nineteenth-century German exegetists, however, placed its writing when David was being persecuted by Saul. Saul was angry and wanted David captured or killed. Accusations had been made against him. David was separated from his family. Jewish commentators see this Psalm's main theme as exile. They direct our attention to the history of Israel and its many periods of exile, and this is identified by David through his own personal exile and isolation. This concept will be taken up later in the book to provide some insight into David and his personal plight.

If either of these events were the contributory catalyst that saw this Psalm written, it would be easy to imagine David praying to God in such a manner. He was at his wit's end. There was no security for him. He felt isolated and alone. He prayed to his God. How else was he going to pray to God? He certainly wasn't going to be praying, "Thank you, God, for this little situation that I am in. Bless me." On the contrary, he cried out, "Save me, oh God!" It doesn't come over to me as a silent prayer, either.

It is more like this: "GOD, HELP ME, SAVE ME!" Regardless, circumstances drove David to this point of despair, and either of the situations mentioned earlier could easily had been a catalyst.

In the following paragraphs, I have taken the liberty to highlight particular words and phrases. These words and phrases highlight certain observations made by different writers about David's particular situation and give us some valuable insights.

Derek Kidner[1] saw the Psalm as revealing **a vulnerable man**. Vulnerable in that he "could not shrug off slander, betrayal and self-accusation."

I do not see David as a passive participant in this circumstance. Passivity is never a word that would describe David's relationship with his God. He was full of artistic expression, worked through music, both composing and playing, as well as his poetry. He was often regarded as a worshipper who wore his heart on his sleeve when communicating with God. So to read that David was in a place where he felt that the waters were to his neck and rising, I don't see him accepting his lot in life, and the words he prayed tend to convince me that he did not want to go down without a fight. He was after all Israel's champion, having defeated the Philistine champion Goliath in combat with nothing but a slingshot and a single flat pebble. But as a man, he also had his flaws. David had personal character traits, secrets, if you will, that made him no different to either you or me.

The metaphor of the person caught in rising floodwaters clearly describes **a sense of hopelessness**. John Calvin described this aspect: "the Psalmist represents his condition as so extremely distressing that it brought him even to the brink of despair." It also conveys **an inability to fight** against a force of nature that has so much incredible power, an individual can be tossed about and dealt with in such a ferocious manner that ultimately could cost them their very life. Matthew Henry described the floodwaters as "The waters of affliction, those bitter waters, have come unto my soul, not only threaten my life, but disquiet my mind; they fill my head with perplexing cares and my heart with oppressive grief, so that I cannot enjoy God and myself as I used to do." He went on to describe that the human spirit can bear up under

---

[1] Kidner, *Tyndale Old Testament Commentary – Psalms 1-72*, IVP, p. 245

troubles, but what if the spirit is wounded? This is how he sees David's predicament: he had **a wounded spirit**. The very aspect of not being able to enjoy life in a way that is so common and familiar is quite confronting, especially when we consider when this was penned. In our present age, the human heart seems to be more susceptible to the disquiet of our mind, as Henry wrote it, or is it that in our modern society, we have become more attuned to the human condition? As a result we see it as being given a higher profile, where we have now started to speak more openly at a clinical level and, as a result, we seem to see the condition of the human mind has also increased in its effects on people. Matthew Henry continued: "His thoughts sought for something to confide in, and with which to support his hope, but he found nothing: He sunk in deep mire, where there was no standing, no firm footing; the considerations that used to support and encourage him now failed him, or were out of the way, and he was ready to give himself up for gone. He sought for something to comfort himself with, but found himself in deep waters that overflowed him, overwhelmed him; he was like a sinking drowning man, in such confusion and consternation."

The human condition can be quite resolute when things are going OK or maybe undergoing minor pressures. We can withstand so much more than we realise, but the thought that Matthew Henry conveyed, "what if the spirit is wounded?" places a whole new perspective. Let's think of the two examples that commentators have raised as the catalyst for the Psalm: Saul's pursuit of David and Absalom's rebellion. What impact did either situation have on David? Have either been enough to wound his spirit, causing, as Calvin wrote, distress and bringing him to the brink of despair? Of the two, the one that could have caused the most distress and driven David to a point of despair is Absalom. When we compare the two: David was fleeing from Saul, but in that same time he was amassing support. Pressures? Yes. But to the point of absolute distress? Maybe not. But with Absalom, family issues festered to the point of vengeance and murder. Sections of David's family were in rebellion. Is this the more obvious scenario?

David's plight was clear, and his tone expressed this aspect of mindset that leaves us in no doubt that when the water is to the neck and rising, hopelessness, distress and despair are identifiable for each of us. He was not alone in these feelings.

Given the right variables a stream can become a raging torrent. This can occur by the flash flood where torrential rain causes water to rise at a dramatic rate. Or the resulting flood is the culmination of a gradual build up, where the rain has not fallen in the particular vicinity but farther up in the catchment area. The waters do rise, but over a protracted period of time, however, the consequences can be no less devastating.

The premise of David's prayer through the use of metaphor describes his feelings—his emotions, thoughts and attitudes. The metaphor of the floodwaters provides us, as readers and onlookers, with the context of the whole Psalm. Without its descriptiveness, we would be at a loss as to his otherwise apparent ramblings. Along with context, the metaphor reaches out across the generations and remains distinct and current even in the twenty-first century. We are easily able to put ourselves in David's place and feel some of his pain and anguish from our own personal experiences. We cannot deny that at times we have felt as David felt, and it is on this basis that we will explore the various components of this Psalm in order to better understand ourselves while looking through David's eyes.

The language of Psalm 69, when read in the *New Living Translation*

(NLT), poetically uses this metaphor of floodwaters to describe a state of helplessness.

> Save me, Oh God, for the floodwaters are up to my neck.
> Deeper and deeper I sink into the mire I can't find a foothold
> to stand on
>
> (PSALM 69:1)

The *Amplified Version* includes the phrase "they threaten my life" in his initial prayer. David was crying out for rescue. This again adds to the drama that is unfolding in the Psalmist's life and provides us with a further insight into his state of mind, along with the effect that it was having on him personally. Life, indeed, is a drama and it is playing out in such a dramatic manner. There is a real sense of urgency in his entreaty. David was at his wit's end. He had nowhere else to go. This appears to be his last resort. As if "floodwaters" aren't bad enough, this is life threatening. The pressure that David must had been experiencing to cry out in this manner… Desperate times bring about desperate measures. They can even bring about a determination and a tenacious attitude to press through.

The *Contemporary English Version* commences with the phrase, "God can be trusted," prior to the first verse. This is an interesting statement, given how David then started his prayer. There appears to be a real contradiction in terms and a paradoxical thought emerges by including these words. I acknowledge this statement is made looking at the more positive aspects of the Psalm and is indeed a truth, but it seems to cut right across the way that David then started his dialogue. It is true that regardless of our circumstances, God is for us in that circumstance and can be trusted to see us through our travail. Paradox is indeed the stuff of life.

Peterson, in *The Message*, spoke of "I'm in over my head," and to convey this feeling of helplessness and being in deep water: "I'm going down for the third time" (verse 2). There is a definite air of desperation in how David was praying. This again provides us insight into David's plight, with this imagery of a person either in a flooded stream or in the surf, their hand raised as a sign of distress and their head going under not for the first time but numerous times, with lungs becoming inundated with water; they are beginning to drown. Life itself is in the balance; death is imminent if there is no intervention and a rescue.

The challenge is to first identify and then articulate the emotion. This is not necessarily an easy thing to do. By this I mean if the individual is a quiet and introverted person, there is the added difficulty of communication. This may be a generalisation of terms, as there are some introverted people who can clearly communicate but do not necessarily need to have the comfort of crowds around. Conversely, the extrovert, who is the life of party, has the added challenge of moving from being the life of the party to becoming open and vulnerable to their friends. This can be an extraordinary challenge, as there is a need to recognise that there is a struggle, and because you cannot do this on your own, there is a point of communicating need in order to have support in a time of need.

I can remember as a young person vacationing at what was in those days a small coastal town in Central Queensland. The town was situated on a bluff with the beach below. On the southern edge of town was a creek across which was an island, maybe 200 metres away. Being a tidal creek, it was possible to wade across the creek near its mouth and walk on the island on the opposite shore. I knew this to be true, as many times I had seen people, adults, cross the creek and walk on the pristine-sand beach of the island. I could see them sauntering hand in hand without a care in the world. One day I decided that if the adults could cross the creek and walk on the beach, so could I. The tide was low and I took my first step into the creek, and I started to wade out into the stream. About halfway across, I stepped into a large hole that had been created by the tidal movements of the water. Suddenly, I was no longer in water to my waist, but the water was reaching my chin, and with the outflow of the tide, I was being dragged under, my footing was unsure, and water flowed over my head.

I may have experienced a tidal creek, but the description David provided was of floodwaters. The water was rushing. It was rough, and at times it was washing over his head. The *Contemporary English Version* uses "I am about to be swept under by a mighty flood." While *Young's Literal Translation* uses "I have come into the depths of the waters." It is through this metaphor that David revealed his present state of mind. He described his experience in terms of "the floodwaters up to my neck." Some translations use the English word "soul" to describe where these waters have invaded. "Save me, O God; for the waters are come in unto [my] soul".[2] The soul denotes the very centre of man: his heart, soul—every part of his being is included. The floodwaters signify *tribulations* (Wesley), *calamity* or *danger* (Barnes).

The water is to the neck and it is rising. This invasion is coming into every aspect of life; no part is spared. This is the same with natural floodwaters. They intrude into everything, either by inundation or seepage. In the end the waters get in; nothing is left untouched. Calvin wrote of this aspect. "A man when he falls into an abyss of waters, may prevent for some time the water from entering his body, by stopping

---

[2] Darby

his mouth and his nostrils, but at length, from its being impossible for a human being to live without respiration, suffocation will compel him to let in the waters, and they will penetrate even to the heart. David by this metaphor would intimate, not only that the waters had covered and overwhelmed him, but also that he had been forced to draw them into his body."

This feeling of "to the neck and rising" can be the result of not one particular reason but can emerge because of a variety of reasons. Work pressures, relationship struggles, financial stresses, performance obsessions, feelings of low self-worth, fatigue and prolonged illness can all contribute. This list is by no means exhaustive; rather, it illustrates that there is no single source or contributing factor. In the end, this list itself may be as long as there are people living on this earth.

Of this passage, John Gill wrote: [it] "signifies not despair of mind, but difficult and distressed circumstances." Seemingly, the metaphor would have us believe that the distress is from another source and not a battle within. The key, however, to understanding what we go through during times of struggle against seemingly destructive forces can be found in our thought patterns. The feelings that are exhibited in the emotional struggle of coming to terms with our circumstances at a time when it seems our very lives are in the balance.

There are behaviours, thoughts, feelings, complete with their related physical outcomes, that become evident when the waters are to our neck and rising. These characteristics may well abound when we are either in a state of stress or at the point of being drowned in a raging emotional torrent. This Psalm outlines these clearly through the course of the text. I have summarised all of these in table form at the end of this book as a point of summary and ready reckoner.

When David spoke of being in the floodwaters, he used the imagery of what it was like to be in them. Not only was the water washing over him, but his feet were also sinking into the mud. He was sinking deeper and deeper into the mire. His predicament was being compounded and made far more difficult and precarious by other unseen forces. David's fight had become a battle on more than one front. The struggle was above as well as below, seen as well as unseen. Where did he fight his battle? Was it with the water that was tumbling over him? Or was it with the mud on the bottom of the stream, David was slipping and could not get a good foothold?

I can't find a foothold (NLT).

I sink in the miry depths where there is no foothold (NIV).

David was clear about his predicament. Can you picture it? Can you identify with him? Did he seem to be accurately describing where you are at while you read this? Or maybe you have been in that place at some earlier time in your life?

Not only were the waters rushing around him, but he was also subject to what was under his feet. It was not firm, good as a sure footing but was ground that was waterlogged. Well, it is not earth so much as mud, slosh. This compounded the effects of the water washing over him. There was no firm foothold. The more David struggled, the deeper he sank and the more the water held sway over the upper part of his body. He was nearer to drowning.

By not having a firm foundation, it can exacerbate what we are experiencing. We are fighting on two fronts. One where we are struggling to our maintain balance, and the other where we are struggling to maintain our buoyancy against the trials of life. The difficulty is that when we are in a place akin to being in floodwaters, then there will also be the unseen struggle occurring.

John Calvin wrote of this verse, "I am sunk in deep mire, where there is no standing place. Here he compares his afflictions to a deep sink of mire, where there is still greater danger; for if a man fixes his feet upon a solid bottom, he may raise himself up, there having been many instances in which persons, placing their feet on the bottom, have by a sudden spring emerged and escaped the peril of the waters; but when a man finds himself once sunk in some slough or muddy river, it is all over with him, he has no means of saving himself. [69] The Psalmist adduces additional circumstances in illustration of his afflicted condition. He declares that he was inundated by the flowing of the waters; an expression indicating the disorder and confusion which his distresses and persecutions produced."

David's graphic description clearly shows us his dilemma. He was being choked by the "water." There was the threat of being washed over, being covered over, which is the visible battle. But there was the mud that was soft, gooey, squeezing up between his toes over his feet and up his leg. The struggle was to stay upright, erect against a powerful, overwhelming force while not having any firm foundation below that would assist him with his balance. He could not hold it out if he could not withstand it; he must succumb to it. Using the metaphor as described which of the two, the floodwaters washing over or the softness of the river bed that made him most at peril. Or does the metaphor provide us with the thinking that there are times when we are able to identify one source of danger but there are also hidden forces or circumstances that are also at play that not only threaten us but also exacerbate the former? These are very pertinent questions and observations that may assist us when we are in that very place, where the waters are to our neck and rising.

I have found that my personal faith in God has not been shaken throughout these times. I have pondered that very thought regarding my faith and have not been able to clearly or definitively ascertain a sound reason or conclusion as to why this is the case. Whether it has something to do with knowing no other life than relating in Christian circles and having grown up in them since a young age. I can truthfully testify to the goodness of God in those times even though at times I, too, did not receive answers to my questions.

CHAPTER 2

OVERWHELMED

W hen the waters are to the neck and rising, you feel overwhelmed.

"I am in deep water and the floods overwhelm me"

(PSALM 69:2B)

There is no better way to describe the sense of hopelessness, help-lessness and sheer overwhelming nature of life's circumstances when they have not been addressed than as a flooding torrent. The situation can become so grave that it can be likened to water to the neck and rising. Situations can be seen as floodwaters, which brings the picture that not only are they neck deep, but they are a raging torrent pushing past you. The waters are not calm, so there may be times when they will wash over the face, into the eyes, the ears, the nose and the mouth. They will even cover over completely at times. The floodwaters have such power, they are causing a sense of loss of balance and going com-pletely under them. There is no sure footing—the ground underfoot is saturated, slippery, mushy, gooey mud. The imagery is so strong!

They are waters that are surging.

They are waters that flow over the top and submerge or cover.

They are waters that are relentless.

They are waters that don't seem to have an end.

David's cry in his predicament, as depicted by the floodwaters, has been related as follows: "The plea in effect is this: Lord, I am ready to drown; if ever thou wouldst save a poor perishing servant of thine, save me: my troubles and temptations are too deep for me, I am ready to sink overhead and ears in them, and therefore, Lord, reach hither thy gracious hand, and bear up my head above water, lest otherwise I miscarry. Especially if such extremities continue, the continuance of them may be pleaded." —Thomas Cobbet.

Go with the imagery for a moment. David was feeling in such a position that he likened it to being in floodwaters; his feet were sinking into the mud at the bed of the stream. The waters were getting deeper; as he went under, he was under great duress and he was feeling overwhelmed to the point of being engulfed by the water. His very survival was at stake. The feeling of being overwhelmed, as David described in this Psalm, is real. The metaphor works wonderfully. How often do we turn the news on and see floodwaters in some part of our planet? Or in those telecasts, how often is it that, in the midst of those waters, we see somebody clinging to a branch of a tree, waiting for someone to come out into the raging torrent to rescue them? Topical evidence of this was the news footage of the Queensland floods in 2011. There we saw an inland, tsunami-type event through the city of Toowoomba and the township of Grantham in Lockyer Valley of South East Queensland. Nothing could stand in its path. Cars were tossed about like toys, and there was horrific human tragedy through the loss of countless lives.

We had the opportunity to drive through Grantham several weeks after the devastation, and we were not really prepared for what we observed. That is the type of floodwaters that I am talking about—the struggle for life itself.

This state of being overwhelmed is very real. We can all identify with it. It is very much like waters that threaten to flow over the top and immerse you, concealing you from the outside world, drowning you. The threat to life and limb is very evident. The fact is that we seem to identify with it even if we have not personally experienced it first-hand.

An image that one may associate with may be that of an office clerk. His desk is piled high with files and paperwork. He is shuffling the papers and files from the in-tray to the out-tray via the one clean area on his desk which is immediately in front of him. He finishes a file, closes it and moves it on. *Great, I have accomplished something.* But then stepping out of the elevator with a trolley is the office messenger. He walks along the workstations and stops at the clerk's desk and proceeds to add another twenty files to the trays that are already piled high. This happens at regular intervals during the day. The end of the day approaches and there are more files on his desk than at the start of the day. Continue this over an extended period of time and with seemingly no visible progress, the clerk has feelings of being overwhelmed by his work. There is no satisfaction or a level of accomplishment. It is too much for one person to complete; the task is too great. He crumples under its weight. He cannot go on. He is exhausted.

For a new mother, the image may be a constantly crying infant. The blessing of birth becomes overshadowed by sleep deprivation, soiled nappies as well as the constant crying that wears her down, as she is unable to directly associate with the needs of her baby. Under the stress, it becomes all too much for her; the mum becomes overwhelmed by everything. She feels that she can't go on. As a mother, she feels a failure; therefore, the pressure builds.

The pressures of life may bring us to the point of feeling overwhelmed. We are at breaking point. One more event or action may be all it takes to see us sink below the waters.

When we have feelings of being overwhelmed, they are often accompanied by tears or the feeling that you are on the verge of crying. Pressures build, and someone says something, and the sensations around the eyes, the heat and the slight quiver at the edge of the mouth. Unless you break down and burst out crying in front of them, these may be indistinguishable to your friends and family.

"I am worn out from sobbing. Every night tears drench my bed; my pillow is wet from weeping. My vision is blurred by grief; my eyes are worn out because of all my enemies"

(PSALM 6:6)

David's emotional strain was so pronounced. How he managed his emotions is a study in itself. To see how his feelings were worked out provides us with an insight into the man. There are times in Scripture when he was openly emotional, as in his dancing and ecstasy at the return of the Ark of the Covenant to Jerusalem, but here, here was a man in the privacy of his own bedchamber, crying out to God and weeping so much that he was utterly exhausted his very bed was drenched in his tears.

His exhaustion from sobbing was mixed with blurred vision. His tears were so prolific that his eyes were stinging, and most probably they were swollen by his crying.

"My eyes are straining to see your promises come true. When will you comfort me? I am shriveled like a wineskin in the smoke, exhausted with waiting. But I cling to your principles and obey them. How long must I wait?"

(PSALM 119:82)

Each of the Psalms exhibits a fantastic turn of phrase. Their outright honesty and ability to tell it how it was without the airs and graces must have endeared them to God, the object of many of the Psalms. Their pleas and cries of despair brought pen to paper as they released what was harboured in the depths of their beings. "I am shrivelled like a wineskin in the smoke..." is very descriptive stuff. Not much is left to the imagination. I have been used up all my life and suppleness has been sucked out of me. But his questions also carry great depth of thought.

They each relate to anticipated intervention from God:

"When will you comfort me?
"How long must I wait?"

God, I know that you are true to your promises, but when? I am really straining my eyes, God. I may be like that wineskin, God, dried and cracked, scarred by my environment, yet I am hanging in there, but how much longer? I know you are coming to help me. My fingertips are digging in. I'm hanging by the skin of my teeth. Please come, God!

Many times we place a time frame on God. Our economies of time are much different. Our circumstances bring us near to breaking point, to the very brink, and we seek respite. Respite from the pain and torment. Respite from the pressure. Respite from the waters that are lapping at our chins and threatening to inundate us.

Our society has conditioned and socialised us that we can have it now! Society says we have a right to our dreams, and anything that gets in the way of us achieving them is brushed aside, or at least minimised as being a mere inconvenience. So when we experience something of the magnitude of David's plight, we are way out of our depth and do not have the emotional capacity to manage, let alone overcome such difficulty. We treat God like He is on speed dial and expect Him to answer now and are not able to handle a time lag in response. We view this as God not loving us or caring enough to provide us with either an answer or, better still, a solution to the issue at hand.

CHAPTER 3

EXHAUSTION

When the waters are to the neck and rising, you become exhausted.

> "I am exhausted from crying for help; My throat is parched and dry. My eyes are swollen with weeping, waiting for my God to help me"
>
> (PSALM 69:3)

Physical exhaustion brought about by a feeling of being overwhelmed by life's circumstances, with those floodwaters crashing in, is not uncommon. David was expressing this struggle that he was in where his life was on the very edge. Often this struggle is fought in private. No one knows that there is even a battle going on. The cries of anguish and for respite are not heard, and as a result of this constant onslaught, a person can become extremely tired. They are in such a weak state—a state of extreme physical or mental tiredness or collapse that the struggle threatens to totally overcome them.

In the previous chapter, I referred to a passage from Psalm 6:6 which is very similar in its subject matter. David had continued in this pressured state to the point of absolute exhaustion. Remember the context of continual floodwaters pressing in and threatening to overwhelm him and the very struggle that this associates. David's state in prayer pleading for God to intervene was such that there was a complete sense of weariness and exhaustion. David's sufferings have been such that under their weight he had become "faint."

The danger for individuals when in an emotional state such as the theme of this book is internalisation. Isolation can become both a safe refuge and also a barrier to recovery, each at the same time. Because of the tendency to exhibit a strong front for the masses, the outcome is to isolate all and sundry while suffering alone and in silence. Without having an outlet, the silence further alienates others and builds up the pressures of stress, and a vicious cycle begins and continues. Internalisation does not offer emotional release and, as a consequence, as it were, emotional bile can start to accumulate. Therefore, the danger is to suffer alone and in silence, or as David did, to raise our complaint to God. I don't know whether this is human nature, but our prayers become our only cries for help.

David spoke of his throat being parched and dry. His crying out for rescue had been such that his throat had dried. His throat became hoarse, his voice would be strained. The Hebrew word used here denotes "to burn, to enkindle and then to be inflamed." The very sense of the excessive exertion of his voice resulted in his throat to become parched so that he could not speak. The constant pressure and the cries for relief left him physically exhausted. There was barely any fight left in him. Exhaustion can exacerbate our situation. The constant pressure of fighting the emotional roller coaster can be draining. Tiredness and fatigue are the real enemies at this time, when the water is to the neck and rising.

When we are in such a state of crying out to God, all our emotional energy is directed towards it. Physically, we may indeed shed copious amounts of tears. The pressure that the situation brings to bear may cause us to release some of that pent-up energy through the physical act of crying. Our bodies are affected by constant pressure, as likened by the situation outlined by David. Prolonged physical arousal, produced by sustained stress, taxes the body. In many situations arousal is adaptive; too little arousal may be as disruptive as extremely light levels.[3] We suffer exhaustion and the effects are so negative. The extreme highs and conversely extreme lows have the same physical effects, positively and negatively, on our bodies. The same amount of energy is dispensed either through an emotional high or emotional low.

As a direct consequence of this emotional state, David's eyes were swollen from crying. When there is a feeling of being overwhelmed, those tears are not far away. Your emotions are on a knife edge. At any moment, the dam of emotion will burst its banks and the reservoir rush out. It is a strange feeling to have your emotions at such a point that almost any minor infraction has the potential to cause the tears to flow. In that moment, the tears seem such an overreaction to stunned onlookers. I know this feeling well. Your emotions are in such a state where the inner struggle has been building, and you can feel as though the tears are coming. Your eyes feel hot and stinging. You are on edge. The slightest sideways look from a colleague or a random remark can cause the final burst of tears or the move away, so those tears can be shed in private.

This example is when the emotions have been "ambushed"

---

[3] David G. Myers p. 374

unwittingly and there is this outpouring of tears and emotions. More often than not the tears are shed in private, far from other people. This is a truly personal battle against the odds. Seemingly no other person knows of this struggle.

David wanted God to help him. He wanted his Deliverer to rescue him; he waited for it. His thinking might have been, *When God rescues me, my pain and anguish and this feeling of going under this wave of torment will be far behind me. I will not have to experience this any longer.* Our thinking becomes so focussed on our predicament that we do not see anything else. We become preoccupied and the battle of our plight leads to our total exhaustion.

We become weary as a combined result of our crying out to God and our emotional state. Have you noticed that when you are in the depths of despair and crying constantly that you become exhausted? People often cry themselves to sleep, whether this is a short circuit of our emotions or it brings out the fact that emotions drain our energy. To emotionally endure something that can be likened to drowning in a raging torrent pushes us to extremes that drain our energy and have a dramatic effect on our demeanour and outlook of the world in general.

Matthew Henry wrote in his *Commentary of the Whole Bible*: "Though he could not keep his head above water, yet he cried to his God, and the more death was in his view the more life was in his prayers; yet he had not immediately an answer of peace given in, no, nor so much of that support and comfort in praying which God's people used to have; so that he was almost weary of crying, grew hoarse, and his throat so dried that he could cry no more. Nor had he his wonted satisfaction in believing, hoping, and expecting relief: My eyes fail while I wait for my God; he had almost looked his eyes out, in expectation of deliverance. Yet his pleading this with God is an indication that he is resolved not to give up believing and praying. His throat is dried, but his heart is not; his eyes fail, but his faith does not."

Matthew Henry's statements provide us with further insight into David's plight. He is one of very few writers that I read who made mention of the floodwaters by way of metaphor. This is in part on the basis of the contents of verse three, by showing David's perseverance in spite of his plight and the strength of his faith in God. This was despite the pressures of the waters being to the neck and threatening to take his life in a metaphorical sense.

I also do enjoy the phrase "the more death is in his view the more life was in his prayers," and typifies Matthew Henry's devotional manner of Bible commentary. He tapped into David's desire to not only survive his present predicament but also to see his God intervene on his behalf. As we continue to read the Psalm, we are left with the unanswered question, was David's plea for help ever answered? Only God knows the answer to that question because neither this nor David's other Psalms provide us with additional clarification, either. So where does that leave each of us? Can we receive some comfort from David's writings or are we "condemned" to a life of unanswered questions? Well, unanswered on this side of glory at least.

The value that Matthew Henry attributed to David's prayer for deliverance can be found in the latter part of the quote where he indicated that "His throat is dried, but his heart is not; his eyes fail, but his faith does not." Under extreme duress, our physical bodies succumb to the elements, but Matthew Henry expressed that within us the spiritual aspects do not faint. Faith is full of resolve and our hearts have not failed us. The sheer tenacity and determination to persevere in the spiritual and not to give up in either believing or praying gives us a glimpse into the character of David. He was not about to be swayed even though, in essence, his life was in the balance. Physically, David's voice was hoarse from crying out and his eyes failed him from the strain of seeking out God's deliverance, but this did not dissuade him. His heart was full. There was still a hope.

CHAPTER 4

Detested

When the waters are to your neck and rising, you feel that people detest you; that they hate you.

> "Those who hate me without cause are more numerous than the hairs on my head"
>
> (Psalm 69:4a)

Hate may seem a harsh word, but when you are in a place that is so unsafe for you, both at a physical and emotional level, no better word can be used to describe it. To feel that you are up against the whole world is not a nice feeling. There also doesn't seem to be a reason for it—well, none that may spring readily to mind.

Nothing is more debilitating to us than our own perceptions, especially when they are founded on either suspicion or speculation. We begin to believe our own "mail" that others do indeed hate us. That perception becomes our reality. Rightly or wrongly we can border on being paranoid. We feel that people are out to get us and do us harm.

We cannot see a reason for their actions. We begin to feel that the people patting us on the back are only looking for a spot to insert the knife. We believe that everyone against us are so many, that they are "more numerous than the hairs on my head." Now this might be a fantastic application of hyperbole but also speaks directly to David's mindset at this particular point in time. In the midst of negativity and pessimism, we often do feel that everyone—the world, in fact—is conspiring against us. This further adds to that sense of isolation and aloneness.

When those feelings pervade our lives we begin to doubt whether we are of any worth. Our sense of value takes a savage beating and is hugely decimated by what we feel are people's opinions of us. David felt that those who hated him were nothing but sneaks and liars. No good thing was going to come out of their intent and he believed that serious harm was on their agenda. As David relayed it, the number of people who hated him was numerous, so many, in fact, that they were more than the hairs on his head.

As king he would have had his detractors and people who would be against him, but here it is as if it was all and sundry. The sense that David conveyed here was that there was no just cause or reason for people to be out to get him. Neither was there any apparent provocation on his part that would engender the kind of hatred that he was feeling from others. Numerous times throughout his life, David experienced this feeling of being hated. It did not seem justifiable to be the innocent party in a one-way hate fest. The language conveys that this is not just a mild dislike, but a hatred that is aimed specifically at causing immense harm.

How do we come to terms with this? To know that there are those who hate us so much is unexplainable, and that their number seems countless, more than the hairs on my head.

To be in that place where hatred is directed towards you, when people's sole focus is to bring about your downfall, can be very distressing. Agendas are such that there is a concerted effort, with the primary purpose of destroying and wreaking havoc.

Psalm 39 resonates with similar themes as our text.

"I did them no wrong, but they laid a trap for me. I did them no wrong, but they dug a pit to catch me"

(Psalm 35:7, NLT)

The ideas of traps and pits speak of hidden perils that are only revealed when either the snare has been triggered or something/someone has walked onto the pit, causing a collapse. Sinister motives carefully planned and executed are the devices of those who are intent on causing harm and injury. Now multiply that by countless people and not just the one and we begin to see the enormity of the pressure that was applied on David.

"Don't let my treacherous enemies rejoice over my defeat. Don't let those who hate me without cause gloat over my sorrows. They don't talk of peace; they plot against innocent people who mind their own business. They shout. 'Aha! Aha! With our own eyes we saw him do it!'"

(Psalm 35:19–21, NLT)

David expressed this theme in a number of other places throughout the Psalms. I have included several as expressed by three translators to show exactly what David was experiencing.

"Consider my enemies, for they are many; And they hate me with cruel hatred"

(Psalm 25:19, NKJV)

"See how many enemies I have and how viciously they hate me"

(Psalm 25:19, NLT)

"Consider my enemies, for they abound; they hate me with cruel hatred"

(Psalm 25:19, AMP)

"Do not deliver me to the will of adversaries; For false witnesses has risen against me, And such as breathe out violence"

(Psalm 27:12, NKJV)

"Do not let me fall into their hands. For they accuse me of things I've never done; with every breath they threaten me with violence"

(Psalm 27:12, NLT)

"Give me not up to the will of my adversaries, for false witnesses have risen up against me; they breathe out cruelty and violence"

(Psalm 27:12, AMP)

"But my enemies are vigorous, and they are strong; And those who hate me wrongfully have multiplied"

(Psalm 38:19, NKJV)

"I have many aggressive enemies; they hate me without reason"

(Psalm 38:19, NLT)

"But my enemies are vigorous and strong, and those who have me wrongfully are multiplied"

(Psalm 38:19, AMP)

"All who hate me whisper together against me; Against me they devise my hurt"

(Psalm 41:7, NKJV)

"All who hate me whisper about me, imagining the worst"

(Psalm 41:7, NLT)

"All who hate me whisper together about me; against me do they devise my hurt [imagining the worst for me]"

(Psalm 41:7, AMP)

"Because of the voice of the enemy, because of the oppression and threats of the wicked; for they cast trouble upon me, and in wrath they persecute me"

(Psalm 55:3, NKJV)

"My enemies shout at me, making loud and wicked threats. They bring trouble on me and angrily hunt me down"

(Psalm 55:3, NLT)

"[And I am distracted] at the noise of the enemy, because of the oppression and threats of the wicked; for they cast trouble upon me, and in wrath they persecute me"

(Psalm 55:3, AMP)

"Show me a sign for good, That those who have me may see it and be ashamed, Because You, Lord, have helped me and comforted me"

(Psalm 86:17, NKJV)

"Send me a sign or your favour. Then those who hate me will be put to shame, for you, O Lord, help and comfort me"

(Psalm 86:17, NLT)

"Show me a sign of [Your evident] goodwill and favour, that those who hate me may see it and be put to shame, because You, Lord, [will show Your approval of me when You] help and comfort me"

(Psalm 86:17, AMP)

These translations use words like vigorous, strong and aggressive to describe how David viewed his accusers. Their hatred was cruel, or they viciously hated him as being the intent, but their actions were wrongful and without reason. By drawing comments, whether fact or fiction, out into the public domain, the intent is to scandalise and slander for no other reason than to wreak havoc and for personal devastation.

CHAPTER 5

ACCUSED

W hen the waters are to your neck and rising, you feel as though you are being accused.

"You are to blame." "It is all your fault!" These are the catch cries that permeate our minds.

> "These enemies who seek to destroy me are doing so without
> cause. They attack me with lies, Demanding that I give back
> what I didn't steal"
>
> (PSALM 69:4B)

This is a constant battle going on in our minds. The feeling that the predicament we are in is all our fault can be very real, and the flow-on effect to family and friends sometimes does not leave us in a safe place of thinking. When we are being pressured as if we are in the floodwaters and having that sense of liability can be a huge burden to carry. We take the attacks as a personal affront, an attack on our very being.

David's experience was that he felt that his opponents were blaming him without cause. To know that our enemies are attacking our very integrity can be quite a harrowing experience. To be at our lowest point and have that occur has aspects of kicking a man while he is down and only magnifies the effect.

Demands are made on us; unfair demands. Our very integrity is called into question. Untruths are unfairly levelled at us. Hatred of this magnitude is always aimed at the destruction of the person who is hated. Total annihilation is the aim. There are no half measures or an aim of just inflicting some suffering.

Matthew Henry wrote, "We are apt to use this in justification of our passion against those that hate us, that we never gave them cause to hate us. But it is rather an argument why we should bear it patiently, because then we suffer as Christ did, and may then expect that God will give us redress." Matthew Henry brought in a thought here that this form of suffering, when endured in the same attitude as Christ by not retaliating or defending our position and screaming against injustice, will place us in the position that will allow God the opportunity to fight our cause.

Charles Spurgeon wrote of this verse: "Usually, when the ruler sins the people suffer, but here the proverb is reversed—the sheep go astray, and their wanderings are laid at the Shepherd's door." Spurgeon was exploring the concept of internal political strife, where the general populace rises against its leader, in this case the king, for no apparent reason and blame is levelled squarely with the leader.

The common thread in these statements, written in very different generations, is that David's treatment was both harsh and unjust, and this is borne out in the statement, "without cause." False allegations are difficult to defend when the assault is brutal and aimed at bringing about total personal destruction. Peterson, in *The Message*, called them sneaks and liars, to identify those who are falsely spreading accusations.

When those accusations are founded solely on lies and fabrications, it can become very easy to want to defend ourselves and rise up against this injustice. To be placed in that position, when the water is to the neck and rising, is an almost untenable situation. Not only are we fighting a personal battle of survival, but this external assault could be viewed as an attack coming from a second front. For us to be in this place of deep, personal struggle and to also have to be on the receiving end of such an invidious attack on our very person, can only add to the trauma and be almost too much to bear.

The accusations are such that, even though you are innocent on all counts, there is a loud call for restitution.

Matthew Henry continued: "Applying this to David, it was what his enemies compelled him to (they made him suffer for that offence which he had never been guilty of); and it was what he consented to, that, if possible, he might pacify them and make them to be at peace with him. He might have insisted upon the laws of justice and honour, the former not requiring and the latter commonly thought to forbid the restoring of that which we took not away, for that is to wrong ourselves both in our wealth and in our reputation. Yet the case may be such sometimes that it may become our duty."

Let's unpack what is being said in this statement. David did have a defendable argument against the unjust accusations of his enemies. Henry alluded to laws of justice and honour that would have proven the allegations as false, so rather than pursue personal justice, David sought a peaceful resolution by acceding to their unjust demands.

From a legal perspective, David was **not required** to make restitution to his accusers. **The law, in fact,** *forbade* this form of restitution, as it placed at jeopardy both his wealth and personal reputation. In my mind, David was potentially setting himself up for major personal loss. It is difficult to imagine what David was going through at this time. His accusers were many, the number of which more numerous that the hairs on his head. They were all out to destroy him, no matter that their accusations were without foundation. The word used here that is translated as "destroy" and has the meaning of extirpate. The dictionary meaning is: to remove completely, destroy totally, root out or eradicate. The intent is to totally remove by inflicting as much personal financial and physical pain. This was clearly a well-devised plan and very deliberate in its intent and execution. David was clear in that his accusers' assertions were without cause; they had no basis either in fact or substance, yet he paid the cost.

But here in this environment of falsehood, we saw David restoring that which he didn't take away. Despite everything, David sought a peaceful resolution from parties who did not appear to have any other negotiating position than his total financial destitution and personal destruction. John Wesley, in his *Notes on the Bible*, wrote that for peace sake, David restored even that which he had not taken through the illegal act of stealing.

It is at this point many of the various commentators that I have read drew a comparison with Jesus Christ. Jesus was falsely accused and, through the conspiracy of the religious leaders of His day, was brought before Pontius Pilate. It is worth noting that Pilate could not find grounds for a guilty verdict based upon the evidence that was presented to him. The very act of Pilate washing his hands typifies this position of unjust accusation. Pilate's act was to distance himself from upholding an unjust conviction with the ultimate penalty given to Christ, death on a Roman cross.

As with Psalm 69:4, where David made restoration, so did Christ in His taking upon Himself the sins of mankind in an act of total selflessness that would restore to us the relationship that was lost through the very first sinful act of Adam and Eve in the garden. To see the larger picture of the redemption, it gives us a greater appreciation of the work of Christ. He thought it not robbery to be equal with God (Philippians 2:6 and 7) and took upon Himself of no reputation the form of a servant and made Himself obedient unto death.

Yes, we can draw some comparisons between David and Christ, but there are significant contrasts as well. Jesus willingly placed Himself into His position to bring about a redemptive act. Christ's act of willingness to repay the cost through His own death, whereas David's recompense seems to be financial and loss of reputation. **Jesus freely gave Himself in my place to pay the debt of sin** that had been passed on from generation to generation from Adam, my forefather, to me.

Having gained some insight into what David wrote in this Psalm and also seeing the example of Christ, one question remains to be asked of each of us. How do **we** respond when accusations are made against us? The intent may not be quite as dramatic as in David's instance, but there may be some loss of personal reputation. Furthermore, do we react in a positive or negative way? Generally speaking, these forms of attack come upon us at the most emotionally inconvenient time, and this is apparent with David's writings in Psalm 69. We are drained emotionally and have very few resources to defend ourselves.

So how do you deal with it? Think for a moment. Do you exhibit the same "heart" as David and bring about restoration even though the cost to you is considerably greater than what would reasonably be expected? To me, in my limited understanding, this concept does not differ much from the teaching of Jesus in Matthew 5:38–40.

"You have heard the law that says the punishment must match the injury: 'An eye for an eye, and a tooth for a tooth.' But I say, do not resist an evil person! If someone slaps you on the right cheek, offer the other cheek also. If you are sued in court and your shirt is taken from you, give your coat, too."

This passage brings to light the natural reaction to injustice—to wreak revenge upon the perpetrator or accuser—but the spiritual or Godly response is not through vengeance or negative reaction but restoration that costs. We could quite easily justify our responses even if we rose up and argued our point.

Based upon David's text, we see that the cost to him was of a financial nature. His accusers' intent rendered him potentially financially destitute. But in spiritual terms, they were not been able to achieve what the floodwaters had not, either, and that was to make him spiritually destitute. To be in a place of emotional endangerment, yet to not have lost our belief in what God can do despite those circumstances, is testament to a sound grounding in Him. To be at the end of the process and to still hold firmly on to faith and to have it clutched firmly in your grasp is the true testimony to the graciousness of God.

"Malicious witnesses testify against me. They accuse me of crimes I know nothing about. They repay me evil for good. I am sick with despair."

(PSALM 35:11–12, NLT)

The very pressure that is brought to bear through fabrications takes a personal toll. Our health can be directly affected by the pressures of accusations brought about with the sole aim of causing personal devastation. This is especially true if our energies and waking moments are consumed by the pressures brought to bear upon us. We compound the effect and self-perpetuate the outcome.

"But they are glad now that I am in trouble; they gleefully join together against me. I am attacked by people I don't even know; they slander me constantly. They mock me and call me names; They snarl at me"

(PSALM 35:15–16, NLT)

Once his lies have taken flight, there is the sheer delight of the pain that is inflicted. A pack mentality appears where even unknown persons also begin to throw about accusations. They pick up the theme and then expand upon it, and can even be more hurtful and vindictive.

CHAPTER 6

FEELING FOOLISH

When the waters are to the neck and rising, you experience a feeling of foolishness.

> "O God, you know how foolish I am; my sins cannot be hidden from you"
>
> (PSALM 69:5)

Foolishness can be a state of mind. When emotions are at their limit, there can be a real and sustained feeling of foolishness: foolishness at feeling emotionally drained; foolish for not understanding the situation we are experiencing. This foolishness can extend to the experience of having to express seeming weaknesses with others.

David did equate his foolishness with a sinful state. The stanza that contains verse 5 draws the two thoughts together, foolishness and sins, or as some translators have written, guilt. David could not hide anything from God. Every sin ever committed is known by God.

The known, the hidden, the suppressed and the forgotten sins are all known to God. David's life was an open book to his Creator.

Now I am not saying that when the water is to your neck and rising that you must be in sin. Sadly, there are Christians who would have you believe that, often, trials and tribulations are primarily the result of sin in our lives. In some instances, this may indeed be the case, but in general it is not in the interests of the person to make a direct connection between trials and tribulations and sinful activity or sinfulness. When you see what some people have to endure in their suffering, it is blatantly unfair to also add the "sinning" label on top. How can we sit in judgement over someone who is experiencing such a dismal life that they feel so overwhelmed? We are so well meaning at times that we quite ignorantly offer solutions to life's problems and call it "in sin." We would rather take the easy way out and give this thing a label and be done with it rather than take the time to understand a person's predicament.

If, as you read this, you have been guilty of believing that about other people, please change your opinions now. They have had the misfortune of enduring the stigma of being made to feel unworthy, and this is unfair. To be judged in such a way is demeaning and does not bring glory to God or His house, the church.

As this verse says, God knows our hearts; nothing is hidden from Him. It is only God and me who really know my heart and therefore are in a position to make the statement that it must be sin. Never ever judge a person when they are going through a time of trial. Firstly, it is not fair on them, and secondly, remember how you judge will be judged back to you. I don't say those as my words; it is found in the Word of God.

God, You know all about me; my thoughts, my dreams, even the number of hairs on my head. You knew me when I was in my mother's womb. You knew me before You created the heavens and the earth; You dreamed of me then. You take a special interest in me, O God. What a blessing to know that the Lord and Maker of all the heavens and earth would take a specific and special interest in me. There is also a description of not being able to get away from the love of God. To not feel foolish needs to be addressed and overcome. To overcome the fear of being judged for such feelings is paramount.

> "For you look deep within the mind and heart, O righteous God"
>
> (PSALM 7:9B, NLT)

God *tests* (NKJV), *tries* (NASB), *probes* (NIV) our hearts and minds. He intimately knows the contents of our hearts; therefore, nothing is hidden from Him. My heart reflects my true self. Jesus took up this thought in Luke 6:45: "for out of the abundance of my heart my mouth speaks." Our hearts are said to be full and described as being full of treasures. Now those treasures are either good or evil, and it is that treasure trove within our hearts that is expressed either through something that is honourable and intrinsically good or wicked and intrinsically evil. Our tongues are the spillway to the reservoirs of our hearts. It is out of that abundance or superabundance that which is contained in there is brought forth, either for good or for evil. The vista that God sees is our hearts in its truest form and our foolishness is not hidden in any way.

Some of the translations I have read use the word "folly" rather than the more modern word of "foolishness." Folly or foolishness is very much about an action that has an element of silliness or unwise conduct. To see our actions illuminated by God's light and knowledge, foolishness is probably an appropriate word. To be viewed by the Creator of the universe, who is also our God and Maker, then everything we say, think or do would have elements of foolishness about it.

Webster's Dictionary defines the word folly as being the fact or state of being foolish. Therefore, folly or foolishness can either be a matter of indisputable fact or is implied by our actions. To see how David moved from a position of not being in the wrong when it came to his situation to a position of being foolish and guilty of things only God knew about is fascinating in itself. The accusations that came David's way, which caused him much anxiety and cost him in a financial sense, did not change his personal belief that, yes, he did silly things, and, yes, when compared to God, he was foolish either in fact or by implication. The spotlight of God's graciousness illuminates our shortcomings, and we have a sense of our humanity and, yes, we have fallen short of His divine plan for mankind. When we are confronted by God, our sinfulness becomes evident.

CHAPTER 7

There Is Still Care for Others

When the waters are to your neck and rising, there is still a capacity to care for others.

"Don't let those who trust in you stumble because of me, O Sovereign Lord Almighty. Don't let them to be humiliated, O God of Israel"

(Psalm 69:6)

This may sound bizarre, but even when we are at out lowest point there can still be the capacity to consider others.

David was experiencing this low point in his life and yet he was showing concern for others that they would not stumble on his account. The anguish that we see at the start of this Psalm had neither eased nor abated, and yet here he was, concerned that those who trusted in God did not stumble because of him. He didn't want to see them humiliated.

What was it within David that would cause his thoughts to wander to others while in his own depths of despair? From the tone of David's comments this had nothing to do with personal perception or embarrassment regarding his predicament, but a genuine concern that others would not be indirectly affected. It is interesting that John Wesley[4] would remark in his explanatory notes alongside the phrase *for my sake*—"because of my sad disappointments. For if they see me forsaken, they will be discouraged by this example." David did not want to be perceived as being forsaken by God and, for the sake of his subjects, to be seen as a stumbling block to their faith and be discouraged as a result. When we are in waters to the neck and rising, we do not want others to suffer because of our own confusion and shame.

Confusion: because we do not understand what we are actually going through at the time. Shame: because our perception of self has been eroded and we are in a position where we have no control. We are brought low by the circumstances, and for others to view us in this way and time is almost too much to bear.

Matthew Henry wrote, "This intimates his fear that if God did not appear for him it would be a discouragement to all other good people and would give his enemies occasion to triumph over them, and his earnest desire that whatever became of him all that seek God, and wait upon him, might be kept in heart and kept in countenance, and might neither be discouraged in themselves nor exposed to contempt from others."

In life we face disappointments—fact. There can also be times when those disappointments have a residual effect. Others are affected.

---

[4] John Wesley's *Explanatory Notes* – website: www.christnotes.org

Leadership is a prime example of this in action. David was a warrior, a leader of men, and yet experiencing a low point in his life. As a leader, you cannot show any outward signs of weakness. Weakness will affect morale. If morale is low, then performance will be affected. If performance is affected, then failure is imminent. Well, that is what society would want to project. Does that make it a valid argument? We will come back to that question.

David didn't want his own disappointments to affect others. He was a warrior among warriors and he was the champion of his followers. He was their king. What a responsibility to bear.

Is This a Portrait of David's Shepherd Heart?

Shepherding his father's flocks was a skill honed in the hills and valleys of his countryside. To be their guide to rich grazing pastures and their protector against animals, the bears and lions that would prey upon the flock.

The passage uses the word "stumble." This gives me a picture of faltering, of being tripped, but it goes much further than that. Other translations express it as being ashamed, disgraced or discouraged. It is not a physical outcome but an emotional one. The flow-on effect can be, in itself, quite devastating. The repercussions can be such that the damage wreaked is of a greater magnitude than the initial.

So How Do We Deal with the Disappointments?

This is a very pertinent question to ask, as it defines who we are. Potentially, we can view this in a positive way, but when the waters are to the neck and rising, the rawness of our emotional state can revert to the negative. The value for each of us personally is to take stock of the disappointment and view it on its own merits rather than "take to heart" the disappointment and further exacerbate our negative self-view. Easier said than done, you may say, but it is at those times when we need to truly examine our own motives and emotions and make a choice as to how we are going to either address the disappointment or dismiss it. It is in this time of analysis that we may need some form of positive external influences to assist in the process.

I come back to the question I posed before. Our natural response is to focus on the negative aspect of performance, and that being contingent upon having it altogether. Leaders lead us but we also have a personal responsibility for our own faith and growth. I am a firm believer in the "priesthood of all believers." I also believe in the principle of spiritual covering. If our faith is contingent upon the success of another or of others, then we are building upon a foundation that is seriously flawed. Leadership does not exclude us from being tested, or to be seen by others to have attained. Firstly, we are human; we experience life like everyone else. For all of us, the genuineness of our faith is tested. The thought I want to convey here is whether it is by "flood" or "fire" that which is of little kingdom value is exterminated, swept away or consumed by flames so that which is of substance is all that is left. It is not the place of testing that is important, but how we come through. That is far more important. We do not learn through our successes, but rather through our failures. Failures teach us where we can do better, or what we can do better. Success can cause us to move our eyes off our God and on to our own success. We do not see room for improvement. You who are in leadership need to convey to your people those times when you have experienced those inner battles as a testimony to the Grace of God and as an encouragement that God is in control and will see them through as He has seen you through.

CHAPTER 8

HUMILIATION

When the waters are to your neck and rising, there are feelings of humiliation.

"For I am mocked and shamed for your sake; humiliation is written all over my face"

(PSALM 69:7)

I do not like feeling humiliated. To have had someone so deride me that I have been left in a state of devastation. Knowing, that seemingly so hopeless to respond while you are struggling with different feelings and emotions can leave us belittled. To have the feeling that there may be someone who has it on their agenda to do you harm by destroying your dignity and sense of worth in such a harsh and mean manner.

David's humiliation was the result of the mocking and shaming that he experienced at the hands of others. He did not see it as his personally, but what he was receiving was on God's behalf; for His sake.

Perceived or real, this is a danger of those who are in that emotional cauldron to hold to that belief.

Another word that describes humiliation is shame. Shame or humiliation is not easy to cover over. Our words, actions, body language and facial demeanour are generally not easy to hide in the presence of others. Our feelings of self are damaged, sometimes irrevocably, without divine intervention.

When someone has been shamed, their head hangs down, eye contact cannot be maintained and shoulders are hunched. These are external examples of how a person may exhibit shame, but there are internal, private demonstrations as well. There may be an increase in blood pressure, your heart races and there can also be a feeling of nausea.

Shame-Based Belief Patterns

When we begin to exhibit signs of shame and humiliation, we also take on shame-based belief patterns. The problem with shame-based belief patterns is that they are founded upon a lie. Over time, we begin to take on the words that have been spoken over us and they gather a life of their own. Any verbal assault upon our person that is designed specifically to harm and bring down a person can only result in a warped opinion of one's self. When a lie is perpetrated on an individual, and then that lie is eventually believed, then the elements of self-worth are eroded to the point where there is little value seen. We begin to see ourselves through the lie and not as we really are. God created us to be valued, to be honoured and held in esteem. We were fashioned in His image; given the breath of His Spirit. This does not make us God but godlike, because we possess within us the very qualities of the creator God. There is a consistent theme in the creation narrative found in Genesis.

> "God saw all that he had made, and it was very good. And there was evening and there was morning – the sixth day"
>
> (GENESIS 1:31, NIV)

> "God looked over everything he had made; it was good, so very good! It was evening, it was morning – Day Six"
>
> (GENESIS 1:31, *THE MESSAGE*)

Two simple words sum up God's view or opinion of you: very good. Capture this truth. God's opinion of you hasn't changed since He surveyed His creation at the end of the sixth day. Neither has the mandate given to Adam been rescinded or taken back. The original blessing has not changed, either.

> "Then God blessed them, and God said to them, 'Be fruitful and multiply; fill the earth and subdue it; have dominion over the fish of the sea, over the birds of the air, and over every living thing that moves on the earth'"
>
> (GENESIS 1:28, NKJV)

God's blessing incorporates fruitfulness, the power to subdue and have dominion, but those who have been subjected to humiliation and shame have been robbed of the blessing of God in its simplest form, because of the lie that you are not worthy. Let me tell you, you are worthy! You are much better than you see yourself. Begin to see yourself as God sees you, as the head and not the tail, above and not beneath, the victor and not the vanquished. God's opinion of us should have a stronger tug on our hearts, but we diminish ourselves through a distorted sense of false humility and miss out on the blessing that God has bestowed on us. God's desire is for us to see ourselves at our very best, and through God's eyes we are good, so very good. The goodness and favour of God are irrefutable, but we reject them because of our mindset. A transformation needs to occur, and that can only occur if we are willing to participate in that process. We need to be changed.

> "I beseech you therefore, brethren, by the mercies of God that you present your bodies as a living sacrifice, holy, acceptable to God, which is your reasonable service. And do not be conformed to this world, but be transformed by the renewing of your mind, that you may prove what is that good and acceptable and perfect will of God"
>
> (ROMANS 12:1–2, NKJV)

A Change of Mindset Is Required

A change of mindset is required. A lifetime of negative talk, negative thought and negative action requires a fundamental change in all aspects of our lives. This "realignment" in our thinking brings us back into conformity with God's view and vision for our lives. It is from that basis that we should begin to no longer be conformed to other people's opinion of us, but to actively engage with God's opinion of us and have our thinking transformed to the glory of God. It is through the act of renewal that the will of God is proved, and it is revealed as being good, as acceptable and perfect. You and I are God's examples and storyboards to this world of His goodness and His grace. We are

his masterpieces. In the previous chapter, Paul laid out the purposes of God, culminating in the following verse:

> "For of Him and through Him and to Him are all things, to whom be glory forever. Amen"
>
> (ROMANS 11:36, NKJV)

Everything, therefore, is of and through Christ. We are to bring our thoughts into captivity and into line with the Word of God. We need to shift our thoughts, intents and actions into line, however how hard that may be to achieve or implement. Be encouraged that the promises of God are yes and amen, so these are low-risk strategies, as the benefits and blessing of God are so much better.

We need to be encouraged that God is mindful of us and cares for our well-being, to the point that He desires to see each of us grow in perfection. This is best demonstrated through God's purposes being worked through Jesus and the cross. We need to grab hold of this truth and appropriate it to our lives—all is Christ. I know that in the event of being in the place where the water is to the neck and rising, it is difficult to be encouraged in that, but my encouragement to you for the moment is to press in to this truth. Begin to be encouraged. Do not let yourself be held down and kept back, but determine in your heart, making the choice to walk in the truth of God's word over your life and appropriate the promises that God has for you.

CHAPTER 9

REJECTION AND ALIENATION

W hen the waters are to the neck and rising, you have a sense of rejection and alienation.

"Even my own brothers pretend they don't know me"

(PSALM 69:8A)

The feeling of utter loneliness, when faced with waters to the neck and it is rising, can be very daunting. To feel that you are so alone; that you have been judged and left to your own devices even by those closest to you. Often, this could not be further from the truth, but this perception has become our reality. Withdrawal from those who are closest to us is a form of self-protection. The thought pattern that "if they knew what I was going through, then they would turn their backs on me and leave me; they would no longer like me." This form of "stinking thinking" corrupts our thinking and distorts our perceptions in such a way that our own personal view of self is "how I think others will see me."

To have that feeling of total abandonment is tragic. Why did David introduce this concept into his prose? Understand that in Middle Eastern culture, family and sense of family are paramount. The family structure forms the basic fabric of its social structure, so to lose that identifier would weigh heavily on any individual, King David included. To have that sense of isolation and rejection from your very own family would not bode well when you are going through an intense emotional time.

This perspective of David's family started to make sense while discussing this in the lounge room of Rabbi Heilbrunn. He brought to light the historical significance of David and the history of his nation and his own family. Why does this have significance in relation to rejection and alienation? Let me explain.

David's grandmother was Ruth, a Moabite woman. The Moabites were the tribe or nation that from time to time crops up in Biblical history. The Israelites camped in Moab on their journey to their promised land and they were also treated harshly by them. There were military conflicts against Moab. Deuteronomy 17:15 stipulates who potentially could be chosen as King—one chosen by God—must be from among the Israelites and not to be a foreigner. The *New King James* uses the phrase, "who is not your brother." Technically speaking, because of Ruth's origin, David was not 100 per cent Israelite. We read in the book of Ruth that she converted to the God of Abraham, Isaac and Jacob when she returned with her mother-in-law Naomi. So by strict definition, David did not qualify to ascend to the throne as king of Israel. It is believed that the book of Ruth was written by Samuel to prove David's "right" to the throne. While David was in hiding from Saul, he went to the king of Moab to make a request, that his mother and father could stay there in safety. What is the relationship that David had with the king of Moab that he would provide sanctuary for David's mother and father? Could it have been through the ancestry of Ruth?

We read that David is the youngest of his family and placed in charge of the family flock. There is some conjecture that he was a shepherd because of the family dynamics. It seems that the dysfunction within the house of Jesse saw David pushed out of the home and into the meadows to tend the sheep. It is not unusual even today for the family dysfunction to play its role in alienating family members. Maybe it's pushing one out into a wilderness area to tend sheep, but emotionally it was not that much different. In the modern context, it could be as inane as sending a child off to boarding school or to a maiden aunt, for instance.

David experienced his own personal exile in these times from his own family, so his was a very personal one. So we begin to understand why he would write in the manner that he did here in verse 8:

"I have become estranged from my brothers and an alien to my mother's sons."

The historical importance of this statement brings to life why he would say what he did. There is a school of thought among Jewish scholars that David was shunted out to the backwoods because of his ancestry, as mentioned earlier. Another thought is that Jesse, at some point, was separated from David's mother and that he had a suspicion that David was not his son, but this is not categorically proven, although there are passages that name Jesse's children who appear to bore out this thought somewhat. To have some form of family dynamic apparent in this family adds to the personal tensions that would have existed. Remember that when Samuel came to the house of Jesse (1

Samuel 16) to anoint a new king of Israel, David was out tending the flocks. He seemed to be a mere afterthought to the family even on such an important occasion. Samuel saw every son of Jesse pass by him but he did not receive God's direction to anoint any of them, and it was only at that point when David's existence was even acknowledged. It was only after Samuel enquired if these were all of Jesse's sons, who had passed before him, that any thought was given to David.

A thought comes to mind here. When David arrived, Samuel rose up and anointed him then left. There was no mention of David being consecrated by Samuel upon his entry, as was the case with Jesse and the seven sons. Samuel simply anointed him with oil. Read the passage. Before Samuel performed the sacrifice he consecrated Jesse and his sons, but at no point was there any mention of this happening with David. The *Orthodox Jewish Bible* says set apart as "kodesh," meaning holy. Each one had to participate in the cleansing ritual or rite before they could be part of the sacrifice that Samuel was going to make to God. This speaks to me in this way: God consecrates an individual regardless of whom man may think or decide may serve in the House of God.

There is one statement that further enhances this concept of unusual family dynamic, and this was made by Eliab, David's elder brother (1 Samuel 17). The occurrence was when Goliath was challenging the army of Israel to mortal combat and to bring about victory for their nation. Eliab's anger was aroused, and he said, "I know your pride and the insolence of your heart." The *King James* says, "The naughtiness of thine heart." Now where does that comment come from? Eliab also had a dig at David about who had been left minding "those few sheep." Even though we can only speculate as to the tone of Eliab's remarks, the fact that there was also anger associated with it can lead us to conclude that this was no isolated incident. Is it the eldest brother of the family showing frustration at the baby of the clan? Or is the remark some form of shame-based rebuke that targets the way David responded to Goliath's taunts and therefore highlights Eliab's fear and reticence to accept the challenge of mortal combat, as was the entire army? There is something to be said for the way that families can conduct themselves, and comments, whether they are shame-based or not, there seems to be a clear indicator to family issues. The level of harshness and the sheer spite and acidity helps draw our conclusion of a definitive conflicted family dynamic. Tensions therefore would not necessarily have been uncommon in this blended family environment.

Marriage in Old Testament times bears little comparison to marriage as we understand it in our lifetime and modern culture. It was not uncommon for a man in ancient times to have more than one wife and to have children born to each one. Even though the household of Jesse seems to have been a minnow in status and wealth, this does not seem to have excluded him from the accepted practices of the period. Scripture shows us that David himself had a number of wives and Solomon is attributed to have had 300 wives and 700 concubines.

Family can be a very "funny" dynamic. Well, for some people, that may be the case, but not mine. No, never mine. To one person, family may be a very positive and fulfilling relationship, but to another it may be the exact opposite: negative and empty. In reality, even within the same family unit a difference of perception as the functionality/dysfunction of the family of origin may exist between siblings. Add to the family dynamic the feelings where the metaphor at the centre of our discussion and the sense of rejection and alienation that may be part of one's existence becomes even more precarious.

It is one thing to have those who are far away from you in a relational sense, who do not really know you, placing ridicule and insult, but when those who are close to you pretend that you are not part of their family, then the sense of rejection is magnified.

Rejection by family can be extremely traumatic and may take many different forms. To one, it may be rejection at birth by a mother. To another, it may be rejection by the family unit because of behavioural issues. And yet to another, it may be rejection borne out of the family dynamic.

Regardless of the form, the same feelings and anxieties will accompany the rejection once it has been identified. There is nothing more tragic than to have a sense of rejection and alienation from the family.

Even though there is conjecture that David experienced alienation in the form outlined earlier, there seems to be a special quality about David's attitude. As children we romanticise David in the fields with the family flock. We imagine he sits there playing his musical instruments while the sheep roam. He is carefree and happy alone, but in reality, he is absent from his family. He has been sent out from them, apparently pushed out of sight based on family dynamics and potential family secrets. A positive in all of this seems to be David's attitude in the midst of all of the family commotion. Nowhere do we see David speaking ill of his father or his family. Position did not hamper David's destiny; in fact, it seems that place of aloneness and solitude defined his character.

The Example of Joseph

Joseph's story shows us a younger son who was also the favourite child of the father. As a consequence, the older brothers took their jealousy to new lows and conspired to sell him into slavery. Initially, they put Joseph down a well, but then the whole situation escalated.

Not only is the rejection seen in the act of selling Joseph into slavery, but then there is a cover-up, the deception that is the result. This form of rejection and alienation may be an extreme, but it illustrates the levels that a family may go. We see with Joseph that there was a very up-and-down pattern of life, but Scripture also shows that his spirit and attitude were not wounded by the various events that saw him elevated to prime ministership in Egypt and later became the source of his family's rescue when famine decimated Palestine. Here, like David's family situation, we see the impact of blended families. Jacob fathered children to two wives, Leah and Rachel, and two concubines, Bilhah and Zilpah. The latter were actually maidservants to his wives.

Scripture shows us how the hand of God weaves itself through the tapestry of individuals' lives and "works" favourably in a plan of redemption, taking what was meant for a negative and making it a positive outcome by the hand of God.

> "And we know that God causes everything to work together
> for the good of those who love God and are called according
> to his purpose for them"
>
> (ROMANS 8:28)

> "Don't you see, you planned evil against me but God used
> those same plans for my good"
>
> (GENESIS 50:20, *THE MESSAGE*)

It could be easy to slip into some romanticised view of the story of Joseph and his family, but Scripture seems to provide the not-so-healthy side of family history which would tend to negate this thought. The history of the sons of Isaac contains deception, rape, vengeance, murder and sexual indiscretion. To me this does not provide a romanticised view of a family; there would be certain portions that you would never want to become public knowledge. It is Joseph's youthful enthusiasm in sharing his dreams with his brothers that set in motion the events that saw the solution to a future problem fulfilled. Other than that there, was nothing that would show that he was a complication in the lifestyle of his family. His heart was pure and his attitude remained intact despite all of the events that conspired to push him down, but as is the law of God, what is made low is exalted. The very same plans that Joseph's brothers had conspired to bring him down a peg or two, God used to turn around a desperate situation and saw a whole family saved from famine.

The Example of Job

The story of Job highlights a situation where he lost all, and even his closest friends forgot him. Job's relatives avoided him. His friends turned against him. Contained in his speech (Job 19: 13–19) are terms such as: rejected by my family, young children despise me, when I stand to speak they turn their backs on me, rejected by my friends and those I have loved have turned against me.

To have endured that type of treatment would be an enormous strain on any individual, but he staggered me when, in verse 25 of that same chapter, he made this incredible statement:

"But as for me, I know my Redeemer lives."

If there was anything that could make a person bitter and twisted, it is the treatment that Job received, but his heart was stayed, and regardless of what occurred or was conspired against him, he knew where his deliverance came from. He talked of a deliverer in the form of a "Redeemer."

You say that, "It was all right for Job, his story isn't like mine." Yes, your story may be different, but the main difference that I can see is that Job's story is chronicled into the most amazing book that there has ever been and yours may be hidden in obscurity and known by maybe only you, and of course, God.

If anyone "deserved" to become bitter and twisted at what happened to him, then Job could win the gold medal. But he wasn't; have a read yourself. His heart stayed true. I don't know whether I would have the same capacity to endure as Job. Well, for a start, I do not want to endure what he endured. I have enough to contend with in my own life as it is. It is those things that put me in a place where, at times, the water is to the neck and rising.

The challenge that is constant can be found in the heart, in the very attitude that exudes despite what circumstance comes their way. To walk away at the end with a pure heart should be our objective, but alas, some of us do not have the capacity to move beyond the hurt and move toward the Healer, and as a consequence we spiral into self-pity, unforgiveness and bitterness. No better example of a pure heart and selfless life than that of Christ's exists.

The Example of Christ

The cross of Christ typifies this sense of alienation from family and brothers. It was on the cross that God the Father turned away from Jesus. Although there were two other men, criminals, who were crucified at the same time, Jesus was very much alone. Isaiah prophesied that "He was despised and rejected." Paul spoke of Christ as the cornerstone that the builders rejected. Scripture tells us that He took upon

Himself the sins of us all on that cross. He bore our shame and received upon Himself our punishment so that we, through Him, might come in eternal life and adoption into the family of God.

It is only through the rejection and alienation of Christ that we have acceptance and citizenship in the family of God. This is a real blessing, to know that on this earth and in your family, you may be rejected and experience alienation to the point that your family disowns you, but that there is a hope, a hope and a spiritual family who will readily accept and support you and provide nurture to a heart and soul that cry out for love and care. Why do they do this? Each of us has experienced some form of rejection in our lives and we know how it feels, whether minor or extreme, in its outworking, but through accepting Christ as our Saviour we receive acceptance and peace that pass all understanding.

You Have Been Chosen

The opposite meaning or antonym of alienation is chosen. Now despite what may be your journey at the moment and the feelings of alienation and rejection that may seem to be part of your present, I want to relay some form of encouragement. God does not alienate us or reject us, but rather He does the opposite—He has chosen us.

Sin by the first Adam separated us from God, but He has provided us with a promise that we will not remain in that place if we would but accept His plan of forgiveness and restoration. That is made available through the Cross of Christ for all who would believe.

Apostle Paul, in writing to the Ephesian Church, said that God chose us before the worlds were made. God chose us in Christ, who stood in our place in order that we would be holy and without fault in His eyes.

God sees us much differently than how we view ourselves. We look at our frailties and weaknesses and faults while He views us through the work of Christ's blood, clean and pure in His sight. No longer are we alienated from God's love because we have been made right in His sight. Grasp what God is saying to you now even as the water is to your neck and rising. Begin to see the hope that is available through Jesus Christ. Believe that He is *your Redeemer*, and that He died on your behalf and now lives as a testimony of the Grace of the Father. Reach out to God in your place of suffering. Believe that He is the Son of God and that He died for your sins.

You are special in God's sight. Begin to see the value that He has placed on you. He gave His Son for you; that is the price that He has placed on you. His one and only Son was given in your place so that you could be restored to Him. God is very aware of your suffering and pain. Reach out to Him; your Redeemer lives and desires a relationship with you. That is what He wants; although God is fully sufficient in His uniqueness, He created a man, Adam, and breathed into him His Spirit. God wanted to share with us the beauty of pure relationship, but as we know the created man was caught in a lie perpetuated by Satan that saw the purity of relationship severed. Man was separated from God but that was not the end of the story. A way was made to restore the right relationship with the Father, and that way is found through the cross of Christ. Grasp this concept! Take a hold of the truth of God's desire to be back in relationship with you.

To some, I may appear to be labouring on this thought, but get it into your spirit, feed on the truth of God's Word, receive your fill. Begin to believe. Belief begins with acceptance!

CHAPTER 10

ISOLATION

When the waters are to the neck and rising, you feel isolated.

"they treat me like a stranger"

(PSALM 69:8B)

A sense of isolation is not unusual when the water is to the neck and rising. Isolation can be our solace or our place of "safety," especially when we have determined that we have been rejected and alienated. There appears to be this natural progression.

Isolation can also be a product of our environment. The very thought that people may think less highly of me can precipitate the need to distance ourselves from family and friends.

Flight becomes our automatic response to those feelings of rejection and alienation. It becomes our default pattern of protection. This mechanism provides self-protection and shields us from the harshness of people's opinions and the verbal attacks that often accompany them.

This sense of being a stranger and isolated engenders the concept that people do not hold you with any form of regard. They do not share an interest in you. You are insignificant in their eyes. There is no consideration of your feelings and this is compounded by the "stranger treatment." Remember that David was charged with caring for the family flock. In a way, he was removed from the presence of the family to undertake an apparently meaningless task, when there would generally be hired shepherds to fulfil the role. History seems to refer to the house of Jesse as being humble and lowly in status, so whether the role of shepherd fell to the youngest in that instance would only be speculative on my part.

Perhaps with this comment David was drawing his sense of isolation to the extent that he was being treated like a foreigner. The effect that this had was perhaps magnified by his predicament. To identify himself as a foreigner seems to be more about a state of mind, where the pressures of life were pressing in such a way that his thoughts and common beliefs were overshadowed by his sense of isolation.

To have the sense or feeling that one does not belong can be devastating to a person. When wrestling with the floodwaters which are to the neck and rising and to feel that you are not part of a larger group, the thoughts of disappointment and societal disconnection can only exacerbate the sense of isolation.

Other than his heritage, as outlined in the previous chapter, and the accompanying family dynamics, we also see that the nature of David's sense of isolation had historical roots. The early books of the Old Testament make specific guidelines to the treatment of strangers or aliens. The way David wrote was of a person who was present physically but excluded from religious and cultural events, a social outcast.

There may be thoughts and feelings that we are misunderstood. Our general demeanour may have an initial impact on other's perceptions of us. Generally speaking, we form an opinion of a person when we first meet them. It may be brought about by the way they dress, their appearance (the way their hair is cut or not cut). This visual summation can often determine whether we begin to engage in conversation with that person. A gruff expression or lack of eye contact can also cause us to form that first opinion, and if we adopt this as our way of initial engagement then we simply compound a sense of isolation, often unfairly at times. This does not need to be person who is quiet and reserved, but often a person who is loud and overt can also drive away communication opportunities because of a perceived embarrassment that can accompany the focus of attention that is associated with it.

There is a perceived stigma associated with this form of isolation. Our society generalises in this day and age so much with people who are isolated and alienated. Frankly we miss the point in our generalisations. We devalue people in our assumptions and presumptions. We totally miss the mark, and the people who are marginalised and disaffected feel totally rejected as a direct result.

Imagine what this would be like for someone with an extroverted personality. A sense of isolation and alienation would be like a dagger to the heart. Not only has the blade pierced the skin, but it has been twisted as well to increase the pain and anguish.

The risk with isolation is we begin to find comfort in our aloneness. Our views are distorted to such an extent that we begin to rationalise and justify to ourselves that it is OK to be alone. No one wants to be around me, they have marginalised me, therefore I will deliberately isolate myself; I am alone, therefore I choose to be alone. This choice is neither good nor is it helpful. Notice I have used the word choose. Isolation is a deliberate choice. Either by the person who chooses to isolate you or you, who chooses to isolate yourself. Regardless of your circumstances that finds you in waters to the neck and rising, you have choices and decisions to make.

CHAPTER 11

THERE IS STILL A PASSION FOR
THE HOUSE OF GOD

When the waters are to the neck and rising, there can still be a
passion for the House of God.

"Passion for your house burns within me"

(PSALM 69:9A)

The interesting thing to note is that even though David was going
through this time where his experience was so very painful, there was
still recognition of a burning desire to serve God. This passion or zeal
was so strong it was as though there was a fire within his belly. He
wrote that it "burns within me," to describe the impact this passion
had on him. This was not about his efforts or desires, but was focused
only for the house of God. There is an element of implied conflict with
David's statement. Here was a man who was struggling for his very
survival, and yet here he was, confessing to God that passion burned

for His House. There was a conscious move on the part of the poet, if only for a brief moment, to look not at his adversity but to look beyond it. Was this reflective on David's part? We do not know. Did David think or have it in his mind that as a compelling argument, this would provide God with a reason to save him from his predicament? Maybe that was his reasoning. Again, we do not know beyond conjecture.

We consider that David's emphasis moved away from his own personal predicament to the flow-on effects upon other people (verse 6). David prayed to God, "Don't let others be ashamed or humiliated because of me." Do not let me be a stumbling block for the faith of others, protect them God. Derek Kidner[5] put it this way: "What will happen to God's people and His name if a servant of His can be insulted with impunity? To feel the force of this, we may picture the dismay of a devoted ambassador (9a), whose country does nothing to protect him from a campaign of humiliation aimed, as he can see, against its own prestige." David knew that, ultimately, the insults and humiliation that he endured were not aimed at him personally, but rather at His God. In verse 9 he wrote, "The insults of those who insult you have fallen on me." At this point, many Bible commentators direct our thoughts to the work of Christ. "It is through the work of the Cross that both parts of this verse are fulfilled. In many ways this context, although valid, has clouded our Christian perception to fully understand David's bewilderment, as distinct from his pain."[6]

I have found in my own personal journey that the passion to assist others was still evident even though my own personal feelings and sadness were at times acute. It is difficult to comprehend but there is an empathy with others who are suffering. I don't know whether it was

---

[5] Tyndale, *Old Testament Commentaries: Psalm 1–72*

[6] Kidner (op. cit.)

because of my own personal pain, but there was an affinity with others that was not there previously. Well, not to the same extent.

John Wesley talked of this passion or zeal as exhausting our spirits. The zeal is that fervent love that is directed at, firstly for God's House, secondly at service, thirdly God's glory and fourthly God's people. Wesley further wrote: "I have been as deeply affected with thy reproaches, as with mine own. This tho' truly belonged to David, yet was also directed by the spirit of God in him, to represent the disposition and condition of Christ in whom it was more fully accomplished, to whom therefore it is implied in the New Testament, the first part of it, John 2:17, and the latter, Romans 15:3."

When there is a God-defined passion for His House, there is an equally powerful drive or impetus to see the House flourish. Nothing will get in the way of the "zealot' in this aspect. The word zealot has been given a really negative connotation through the modern press. Basically, someone who has a powerful devotion to a cause and is full of zeal can be called a zealot, positively or negatively.

This sheer power of this form of devotion saw the disciples reminded of this passage when Jesus cleared the Temple (John 2). The House is a place of worship, and in this context the place of the presence of God, so to see the worship of God reduced to a marketplace with the heart aspect of the worshipped reduced to a financial transaction, the weight of Jesus' passion in driving out the superficial worship of the Lord God saw Him saying:

> "'Get these things out of here. Stop turning my Father's house into a marketplace!' Then his disciples remembered this prophecy from the Scriptures: 'Passion for God's house will consume me"
>
> (JOHN 2:16–17, NLT)

When the waters are to the neck and rising, we can sometimes take on things that are not ours to take on. For some reason we can easily take on the offences that are directed at God and claim them rightly or wrongly as our own personal offence. Whether this is a direct result of our passion for God's house or some other source they seem to fall on us.

Is this because we are emotionally shattered, overwhelmed by the cares of our life that we become vulnerable? Should we take them on? These are pertinent questions to ask ourselves. Well, do we ask ourselves these questions or do we avoid them? The journey to this point is a slow progression. Do we become vulnerable to this effect? In reality these are very difficult questions to answer, as each individual will journey this in vastly different ways. The process of our mind talk will vary for each person, and to acknowledge that we are taking on what isn't ours is not an easy thing to do, firstly to identify that we are doing that, and then once we realise it, to actually set it down in order to deal with our own hurts. In our vulnerability, we should endeavour to take on that which is not ours to take on. Never take on someone else's issues and definitely not those things that are directed at God. Nothing is ever achieved, and our personal healing is impacted and hampered.

Charles Spurgeon, the eminent English preacher of the nineteenth century, spoke of depression in his *Lectures to My Students*. In lecture 11, he talked of the "Minister's Fainting Fits." He began his lecture with this comment: "As it is recorded that David, in the heat of battle, waxed faint, so may it be written of all the servants of the Lord. Fits of depression come over the most of us. Usually cheerful as we may be, we must at intervals be cast down. The strong are not always vigorous, the wise not always ready, the brave not always courageous, and the joyous not always happy." He continued later with the thought: "Immersion in suffering has preceded the baptism of the Holy Ghost. Fasting gives an appetite for the banquet. The Lord is revealed in the backside of the desert, while his servant keepeth the sheep and waits in solitary awe. The wilderness is the way to Canaan. The low valley leads to the towering mountain. Defeat prepares for victory. The raven is sent before the dove. The darkest hour of the night precedes the day-dawn. The mariners go down to the depths, but the next wave makes them mount to the heaven: their soul is melted because of trouble before he bringeth them to their desired haven."

He spoke of a natural progression from low to high, that success or destination is only achieved through the journey. Often, we view the low place or the time of testing as an imposition on our person, where we experience suffering, failure and emotional torment, but Spurgeon was saying that emotional lows are a part of life and ensures us that we are heading in the right direction, our destiny.

Spurgeon listed what he described as a brief catalogue which are favourable to fits of depressions.

- *The hour of great success*
  Seemingly, when there has been great success or some form of achievement, then the resultant aftermath can be a period of lowness.
- *Before any great achievement*
  The wait, at times, can consume our thoughts and cause us to second-guess and bring upon ourselves self-doubt and thoughts of failure.
- *In the midst of a long stretch of unbroken labour*
  When we are constantly on the go and not giving ourselves permission to take some timeout to recharge and

refresh, we can become susceptible to some form of lapse in mental health. Fatigue plays a huge part in bringing about anxiety and depression.

- *One crushing stroke has sometimes laid the minister very low*
  The magnitude of a single event can bring a person low. It may be a personal act of a friend, a betrayal, a dispute that brings division or irreconcilable differences.
- *When troubles multiply*
  The constant weight of prolonged pressure and no remedy/solution being forthcoming can bring about a catalyst for a period of potential depression.

Surgeon's ability to articulate to his students the "perils" of ministry, coming from a place of personal experience, would have been a sobering reminder to care for oneself. Oftentimes energy is devoted to the care of others at our own expense, but we need to understand the principle that self-care will make us more effective in caring for others. Our effectiveness is magnified many times over.

CHAPTER 12

RIDICULED

W hen the waters are to the neck and rising, you feel ridiculed.

"and the insults of those who insult you have fallen on me.
When I weep and fast before the Lord, they scoff at me. When
I dress in sackcloth to show sorrow, they make fun of me. I am
the favourite topic of town gossip, and all the drunkards sing
about me"

(PSALM 69:9–12)

It is not nice to have the feeling that you have been ridiculed. The
primary aim is to degrade and mock in such a way that your sense of
self quality is devalued; to be insulted in such a manner that you are
the recipient of being mocked and shamed. There is also an element of
contempt in the manner that this is produced.

What was David ridiculed for? Matthew Henry identified two
aspects of David's ridicule or reproach. "Reproach was one of the
greatest of his burdens: 'Lord, roll away the reproach, and plead my

cause, for, 1. It is for thee that I am reproached, for serving thee and trusting in thee: For thy sake I have borne reproach. Those that are evil spoken of for well-doing may with a humble confidence leave it to God to bring forth their righteousness as the light. 2. It is with thee that I am reproached: The zeal of thy house has eaten me up, that is, has made me forget myself, and do that which they wickedly turn to my reproach. Those that hate thee and thy house for that reason hate me, because they know how zealously affected I am to it. It is this that has made them ready to eat me up and has eaten up all the love and respect I had among them.' Those that blasphemed God, and spoke ill of his word and ways, did therefore reproach David for believing in his word and walking in his ways. Or it may be construed as an instance of David's zeal for God's house, that he resented all the indignities done to God's name as if they had been done to his own name. He laid to heart all the dishonour done to God and the contempt cast upon religion; these he laid nearer to his heart than any outward troubles of his own. And therefore he had reason to hope God would interest himself in the reproaches cast upon him, because he had always interested himself in the reproaches cast upon God."[7]

What can be drawn from these statements exhibits David's passion and drive where highly focused on His relationship with God. He identified the common source of the derision that he received from his detractors, and it was for God and with God that he bore the burden of his belief and passion.

It didn't matter what David did; they scoffed at him when he wept and fasted, and they made fun of him when he was sorrowful. He was the topic of discussion with the town gossips and the drunks would sing ditties about him. Matthew Henry again wrote, "They ridiculed

---

[7] *Matthew Henry's Commentary on the Whole Bible* (1706)

him for that by which he both humbled himself and honoured God. When men lift up themselves in pride and vainglory they are justly laughed at for their folly; but David chastened his soul, and clothed himself with sackcloth, and from his abasing himself they took occasion to trample upon him. When men dishonour God it is just that their so doing should turn to their dishonour; but when David, purely in devotion to God and to testify his respect to him, wept, and chastened his soul with fasting, and made sackcloth his garment, as humble penitents used to do, instead of commending his devotion and recommending it as a great example of piety, they did all they could both to discourage him in it and to prevent others from following his good example; for that was to his reproach. They laughed at him as a fool for mortifying himself thus; and even for this he became a proverb to them; they made him the common subject of their banter."[8]

When the water is to the neck and rising, you feel that all eyes are upon you and that you are the topic of conversation. This may be true or a believed truth, but in your mind's eye you are the centre of conversation. You feel rightly or wrongly that all eyes are on you and the result appears as with David, that the town drunks sing ditties about you and you are the subject of the town gossips.

When the water is to the neck and rising, there is a sense that your every move is being scrutinised and you are judged for your actions. Colloquially, you are damned if you do and damned if you don't. This added dimension casts a shadow over your demeanour, to the extent that you feel as though you can remain invisible to the talk. In reality you are not necessarily the centre of conversation, but because of heightened personal sensitivity you feel as though that is indeed the case.

---

[8] *Matthew Henry's Commentary on the Whole Bible* (1706)

I cannot remember the source of the following quote: "Though we may be jeered for well-doing, we must never be jeered out of it." Believe this statement with all your being. As you read this, you may indeed be in the floodwaters and you are floundering with the waters to your neck and it's rising fast, but as you cry out to God for His deliverance, do not be jeered out of your faith in Him. The writer of Hebrews implored them:

> "Let us think of ways to motivate one another to acts of love and good works"
>
> (Hebrews 10:24, NLT)

We are tasked to encourage each other—well, really, to be creative in ways of being able to see the potential of others motivated towards well-doing. But people will attack us and jeer us and make accusations against us. They will attack our person, our integrity, our belief system, our faith in an attempt to break us down—to destroy our hope and trust in God. Everyone, regardless of faith, has the capacity to do good things. It is not so much the action but the motivation that comes under attack. Giving selflessly is the heart of the Father. Yes, we are going to come under scrutiny, and as a direct result we will be attacked. The difficulty is when we are at a low point and the attacks come; we have a reduced capacity to deal with them. It is at those times when we must cling most tenaciously to God and stay the course, fight through and not be swayed. The jeering of others, although painful, must never affect us to the extent that we no longer participate in acts of mercy and doing well. Doing well is all about faith in action, and if our faith has no corresponding action, then it is dead.

"So you see, faith by itself isn't enough. Unless it produces good deeds, it is dead and useless"

(JAMES 2:17)

I love one phrase from Bishop T. D. Jakes book *Loose That Man & Let Him Go!* "I am a man of prayer. I will be knocked down no lower than my knees!"[9]

We have bought into a lie that we are not good enough, strong enough or smart enough to know how to deal with our challenges. We capitulate far too easily and do not demonstrate the capacity to fight, but the premise of Bishop Jakes is that we have been created in the image of God and He has predestined each of us for greatness. We need to come into a relationship with God that sees us clinging to Him through a lifestyle of fervent prayer.

There is power in each of these statements; let a positive come out of your dilemma. May it be an opportunity for God to act on your behalf, to bring about His saving, miraculous power breaking into your predicament and bringing the freedom and deliverance that can only occur through His Work.

"Everyone who sees me mocks me. They sneer and shake their heads, saying, Is this the one who relies on the Lord? Then let the Lord save him! If the Lord loves him so much, Let the Lord rescue him"

(PSALM 22:7–8, NLT)

When people know you are a Christian, you may be held to a higher standard. Even though at times this standard may be flawed

---

[9] T. D. Jakes, *Loose That Man & Let Him Go!*

by their worldview, or even by their previous experiences with other Christians, there can be an aspect of unfairness in it. When we are in the place of the floodwaters, the attacks will be directed at our faith. They will try to undermine our belief system and, in their own way, challenge the depth of our faith. The tone of "Is this the one?" is full of spite and venom, with the clear intent of attacking the faith of the victim. The value of the one being verbally assaulted is being minimised with a view of dismissing him entirely. The story of the crucifixion depicts this very same example of derision.

> "He trusted God, so let God rescue him now if he wants him!"
>
> (LUKE 27:43, NLT)

While Christ was on the cross, there was a direct taunt and attack on the message that Jesus spread. In an effort to pull Him down and attack His emotional person, they tried to use His lifestyle and words against Him, but to no avail. Catch this truth. Words may be spoken that are designed and attempt to pull us down and to destroy us, but they do not define who we are.

CHAPTER 13

CRYING OUT TO GOD FOR DELIVERANCE

When the waters are to your neck and rising, you cry out to God for deliverance. You do not want to be going through this. You just want Him to reach down and supernaturally pull you from out of those depths. You want out of there; now not later.

> "But I keep right on praying to you, LORD, hoping this time you will show me favour. In your unfailing love, O God, Answer my prayer with your sure salvation. Pull me out of the mud; Don't let me sink any deeper! Rescue me from those who hate me, And pull me from these deep waters. Don't let the floods overwhelm me, or the deep waters swallow me; or the pit of death devour me"
>
> (PSALM 69:13–15)

It is interesting to note that David used two particular words at this part of his prayer: "this time." By inference we could believe this was not the first time David was in this situation. He was in this place before and it did not make this experience any less painful. David was praying to his God and was determined that come what may, he would keep on praying, hoping that *this time* God would smile down on him and show him His favour.

This Time

Some of the translators described this in terms of the following:

- *Amplified Version*: "At an acceptable and opportune time"
- *Contemporary English Version*: "when the time is right"
- NKJV: "in the acceptable time"
- *The Message*: "God, it's time for a break"
- NIV: "in the time of your favour"
- NLT: "you will show me favour"
- *Young's Literal*: "a time of good pleasure"

We need to understand God's economy and His plan for our lives. Scripture says that His ways are higher than our ways, and His thoughts are higher than our thoughts. So what do we deduce from this? God's timing is perfect in His plan. When we struggle, as with the waters to the neck and rising, we are only looking at our immediate predicament; we do not see the whole picture. To better describe this, it is like we are looking at a specific piece of jigsaw sitting among many others while God is looking at the completed picture. It is pristine; it is perfect. That is how God sees us—perfect, pristine and a thing of beauty to behold.

Neither are the feelings of the waters up to the neck and rising reference a singular event, but appear to allude to something that is more cyclical in nature. David didn't indicate what other times there were when he had this same feeling, but he strongly indicated that this was not the first time. Other psalms support this premise.

David's prayer did not bring with it the concept of repeating something with a view of achieving a different outcome. This is about being in a "same" predicament again, not necessarily of our own choosing, and in that place, we are praying to God: (1) for His favour and (2) for His deliverance—that is, His *sure* salvation. This is not so much about us but about having God enter into our circumstance or situation, where we are otherwise powerless to alter the outcome, and seeing Him work miraculously on our behalf. The only constant here is that we are crying out to God. Today's society is looking for a guarantee and a satisfaction that is based on a WIIFM attitude, "What's in it for me?" But it should be less about me and more about God. It is about the Creator and not the creation. His salvation is sure. It comes without conditions. There is no small print that places stipulations and obscure clauses on us. It is clear, in fact, and unambiguous. It is God, the Lord of the Ages, reaching down through the ages and touching us through His Son. It (salvation) can be said isn't cheap, but it's free.

Favour is an interesting word in a spiritual sense. Here David was praying for the favour of God in his circumstance. So what is the favour of God? What does it look like? Some would describe the favour of God through the little things in life that provide us with blessings—a good parking space in a crowded car park, a job promotion or pay increase. Yes, these can show us the favour of God at work in our lives, but it is in the life-and-death struggles of life where we really want to see God's favour at work. This says to me that we cannot do this on our own, and that we need outside intervention.

God's Sure Salvation Comes through God's Unfailing Love

The phrase "unfailing love" appears twice in this Psalm and a total of seventy-five times throughout the Psalms plus numerous other times in the Bible. The concept of God's love never failing is central to the gospel message. Where in life these are no guarantees, or the concept of faithfulness is constantly being challenged to have a God who loves us unreservedly can bring comfort to the troubled mind.

When the water is to the neck and rising, we should never consider our circumstance as a time of failure or that it is a result of sin. David was conscious of the fact that God is fully aware of our sinfulness—they are not hidden from Him. He sees our hearts, knows our thoughts. But this does not imply that sin has been the catalyst of this being in waters up to the neck and rising. Only as he was praying and crying out to God did he again become conscious of his own sinful state. As we reflect on God and His faithfulness and saving grace, we cannot help but be drawn to our own sinful nature as it becomes "noticeable" in the light of purity. His pure light reveals all that hidden in the dark places and recesses of our hearts.

It is God's unfailing love that reveals His desire to provide us with a sure salvation. There is nothing surer in this world than to be the recipient of the unfailing love of God, when it is revealed through the message of salvation. To receive this is both humbling and liberating at the same time. This is salvation is received despite our sinfulness. David was crying out for the grace of God to be displayed in all of its awesome glory and bring about salvation from the water that was to the neck and rising.

Matthew Henry wrote, "God will not drive us from him, though it is need that drives us to him; nay, it is the more acceptable, because the misery and distress of God's people make them so much the more the objects of his pity: it is seasonable for him to help them when all other helps fail, and they are undone, and feel that they are undone, if he do not help them."[10] This has been my experience, that God does not drive me away when I am at the end of my tether, sinking as it were into the floodwaters. He is there in my time of help.

This is one area where David wanted to see victory and receive favour with and from God.

Know of God's Unfailing Love

Another word for this phrase is lovingkindness. This is an old word, but when used in the following way, "Thy lovingkindness is better than life," we begin to see its importance. It is God's love for us that should be the one thing that can get us through, but in our experience, this is generally not the case. However, God's love is sure.

David now returned to the metaphor of the floodwater. This repetition of metaphor was something that made me look at this psalm from the perspective that I have. The power of the imagery brings to life both the predicament, complete with its potential tragic consequences, and the power of God and its capacity to bring about His salvation. A salvation that is sure, that can be trusted and relied upon. There is no other name under heaven by which we can be saved.

---

[10] Matthew Henry, p

CHAPTER 14

A SENSE THAT GOD HAS FORGOTTEN YOU

W hen the waters are to the neck and rising, you feel as though God has forgotten you.

"Answer my prayers, O LORD, For your unfailing love is wonderful Take care of me, For your mercy is so plentiful. Don't hide from your servant; answer me quickly, for I am in deep trouble! Come and redeem me from my enemies"

(PSALM 69:16–18)

David had a feeling that God had forgotten him; that God had hidden Himself from him. This compounded his feeling of isolation further, as now it was even as though God had abandoned him. He also connected this with "answer me quickly, for I am in deep trouble." David's plight and condition of mind were such that he wanted to convey the extreme peril that he was experiencing. "Please, God, help me here! I don't know how much longer I can go on with this. I'm in deep trouble here. Hey God, I'm over here. Help me!"

Now the feeling was absolute. In his state he had this sense that God had withdrawn from him and he was all alone. "God, let me know you are there for me. Do not delay your response and hear our cries. Come rescue me." Our aloneness becomes deafening. God knows this or He wouldn't have said, "It is not good to be alone," but when the water is to the neck and rising, we do feel the loneliness that He identified.

When the waters are up to the neck, we can feel dryness in the spiritual sense. In fact, sometimes I would go so far as to say that we do not feel anything. Our experience of God becomes the thing most distant from our minds. We are in survival mode. The cares of life have weighed us down and, as a consequence, our demeanour has become clouded and our God-consciousness is affected.

How did this make David feel? More importantly, how does it make me feel today as I read this? We can look at the "other person," in this instance David, and see what was going on in his life, but if we cannot move into the place of pain and identify the "me" in that same situation, then we have missed the point. There are times when we often easily identify with the troubles of others, and then there are other times when we just don't get it. We each have experienced the feeling of aloneness when it comes to the presence of God. For some it is but a short time, yet for others it is a place of perpetual pain.

It is interesting that David prefaced this sense of being forgotten by God with two statements of fact regarding God: that God's unfailing love is wonderful, and God's mercy is plentiful. Not only is His lovingkindness wonderful, but it is good (KJV), sweet and comforting (*Amplified*).

Other scriptures/common theme to our passage:

"My God, my God, why have you abandoned me? Why are you so far away when I groan for help? Every day I call to you, my God, but you do not answer"

(Psalm 22:1; Matt 27:46; Mk 15:34)

O LORD, do not stay far away! You are my strength, come quickly to my aid! Do not turn your back on me. Do not reject your servant in anger. You have always been my helper. Don't leave me now; don't abandon me, O God of my salvation"

(Psalm 27:9)

"I pray to you, O LORD, my rock. Do not turn a deaf ear to me. For if you are silent, I might as well give up and die"

(Psalm 28:1)

"For you are God, my only safe haven. Why have you tossed me aside?"

(Psalm 43:2)

"Listen to my prayer, O God. Do not ignore my cry for help!"

(Psalm 55:1)

"O God, don't stay away. My God, please hurry to help me"

(Psalm 71:12)

The psalmist certainly experienced this feeling of isolation and abandonment on many occasions, as is attested by the preceding verses. This thought of abandonment has an element of "hiding the face" to it. The concept is expressed in Psalm 27:9 and is the thought of turning the face away with displeasure, as if we would not look on one who has offended us. Scripture sometimes uses the term "God lifting His countenance on us" to show us His favour. Contrast this feeling with the following:

> "Where can I go from your Spirit? Or where can I flee from Your presence?"
>
> (PSALM 139:7, NKJV)

Obviously, this is written at a different time and from a vastly different mindset, but it doesn't matter how high we go, into the heavens, or how low we go, even into hell as it were; we cannot get away from God's presence. He is there with us. God has hedged us about, to the front and to the rear, to the left and to the right, and its knowledge is too wonderful. Therefore, what drives us to believe that God has abandoned us? The *New King James* version describes two positions:

- Firstly, turn to me (Psalm 69:16), and
- Secondly, do not hide your face (Psalm 69:17).

In essence, God face me and do not neglect me.

Our next response is to want God to answer us. Intellectually, we know many things about God: His unfailing love and His tender mercy. We know they are both wonderful and plentiful, but when we are in the middle of a traumatic experience, that knowledge is caught up in the moment and we feel that God has somehow abandoned us and we are left to suffer through whatever event/experience that we are going through, alone.

The tragedy that accompanies this mindset of aloneness is that this is not only associated with God. Aloneness extends to our natural everyday environment—in our workplace, at social events and even with family. Tragedy is not too hard a description of this and it is commonplace when someone is in the middle of an event, where the water is to the neck and rising. It matters little whether this sense of aloneness is perception or reality; it matters little that people believe that it is a truth.

I have been fortunate in this aspect, although there have been times when I have chosen to be alone. Throughout, I have been blessed with a wife whose support for me has been outstanding. At those times, when I was at my lowest, she would speak words of encouragement, really speaking into me words of life. Where there was negativity, she would speak positive words. When I chose to separate myself from people, she would spend time with me. It is difficult in that environment to stay downcast for an extended period. The deliberate action that Jenny took in the situation was really a godsend and a tangible demonstration of her love and devotion to me.

CHAPTER 15

BROKEN-HEARTED

W hen the waters are to your neck and rising, you can feel
broken-hearted.

"Their insults have broken my heart, and I am in despair"

(PSALM 69:20A)

Brokenness can take a number of different forms. It can be as the
result of what life has thrown our way or from extreme personal loss.
Here David saw the insults as the catalyst to his brokenness. This sad-
dened his heart and left him in despair. The words spoken were to the
point that they damaged his spirit. The *New Living Translation* word
"insults" is also described as **reproach** (NASB, NKJV), **scorn** (NIV)
and **taunts** (*The Message*). Despair can also be described as **full of
heaviness** (NKJV), **helpless** (NIV), **reduced to nothing** (*The Message*)
and **sick** (NASB). Broken-heartedness brings with it real physical outcomes. Our demeanour can be a real giveaway, especially when it is
the result of a relationship breakdown or as the result of loss of a loved

one, but when our broken-heartedness has been caused by words spoken, then we can try and cover up. But regardless of who we are, there is an upper limit, a place where enough is enough and the next words spoken shatter us completely. The compounding effect of words spoken should never be taken too lightly. At the start we are maybe able to flip it off, but we don't really. Gradually, the residue of constant insults clogs our emotional being and we are brought down dramatically.

Disappointment can bring this about. Loss of relationship can also leave a person with a broken heart.

The cry of the human heart is for relationship, to love and be loved. Our Psalm tells us:

"If only one person would show some pity; if only one would turn and comfort me"

(Psalm 69:20b)

Regardless of who we are, there is something deep within us that craves relationship. It is the cry of the human heart. Many would say that relationship is the meaning of life. Relationship brings fulfilment, completeness, peace and harmony. David was seeking for just one person. He was not after a large number of people, just one. Normally, solace cannot be found in the crowd. The crowd gives us an "out," where we do not have to deal with or address our broken-heartedness. The crowd doesn't allow us to work through the issues at hand so the cry for just one person is justified. One is all it takes for a person to feel accepted and valued. To know that one person has reached out into our aloneness. That extension of themselves is a deliberate choice that is made, and they may not even have an awareness of the inner tumult that is our life. They may just be friendly, it may be purely out of politeness, but someone has reached into our world.

Isaiah's prophecy in chapter 61 speaks of bringing comfort to the broken-hearted. This passage was essentially speaking of Jesus' ministry and, in Luke 4, relates back to this scripture when Jesus was in Nazareth and read from the scroll, saying that this prophecy was now fulfilled. We should also recognise that ministry to the poor, broken-hearted and captive, does not stop with Jesus alone. We, as his representative on earth, as His eyes, hands and feet, should also participate in this ministry.

The Bible tells us that God's DNA is in us.

> "Those who have been born into God's family do make it a practice of sinning, because God's life is in them. So they can't keep on sinning, because they are children of God"
>
> (1 JOHN 3:9, NLT)

As a child is the product of the union of his mother and father and takes on their physical attributes, so do we in a spiritual sense because God breathed life into Adam. We are at the heart of God's desire and creative plan; His very nature is within us. As Apostle John said, His seed, that is, *sperma* (Greek – σηέρμα), the source of life, is in us. How do we know that this is the case? The creation story relates to us the beginning of human life. Adam was just a form until life was breathed into him. The writer of Genesis said that God breathed into man (Genesis 2:7) and became a living being. The language of Genesis chapters 1 and 2 is interesting in that of all the elements that God created, man was the only one where the words "make" and "formed" were used. The others, elements of creation, are spoken into being—"Let there be"—and it was, that is, created. But with mankind, God fashioned him from the dust of the earth and in His image or likeness. There seems to be a special interest in man. Then to provide man with the sense of the union of the triune God, He creates woman from out of man and provides a spiritual and physical connection that is an earthly example of the oneness of God. Woman was created to be a companion to man, to complete him. God saw that loneliness in man and that he was all alone in creation. God's desire was to have relationship with man, not out of a sense of loneliness in Himself but to have the interaction with His created being. In breathing into man, God also breathed into him His creative nature, and we see this with the responsibility of naming the animals of creation being given to Adam.

When the water is to the neck and rising and you are all alone, to have someone come alongside and identify with you can be a real blessing. In his prayers, David cried out to God for deliverance; he had feelings of isolation and detachment, yet there was this desire for someone to recognise his predicament and come alongside, and show compassion and comfort.

How do people know that you are struggling? Because of isolation and this lack of communication regarding feelings, people do not recognise each other's signs of struggle. Often people do not know anything until long after the event, and then still may not recognise the warning signs unless they have been told. This lack of communication exacerbates the isolation and sense of loneliness. We learn to conceal our struggles. We mask our struggles. What a contradiction. We want people to know on the one hand, but on the other we don't want them to know. Modern society has magnified the extent of our isolation with social media outlets readily available on our electronic equipment. Our number of friends is based on our Facebook page or

LinkedIn page, but these are artificial and do fill the need. Yes, they serve a purpose of maintaining contact with friends in other states or countries, but they should never replace the physical human interaction we most crave.

How will people know unless they are told? A common response from people is, "Oh, I didn't know." People can be quite sincere in their ignorance. Often, we are our own biggest enemies. We wear masks to hide our true selves. Our faces bear facades, much like a film set where the front of the building is a beautiful ornate front, but behind that it is nothing more than braces and structural supports.

Why do we do this? If our exterior reflected our inner turmoil, people would not necessarily like what they would see. People are generally drawn to happy people. To have to try to communicate with someone who is broken-hearted is hard work. It is awkward and can be a frustrating conversation. Gloom does not generally engender confidence that you will attract a crowd, not even one or two friends.

Is it perception or is it much more? This is not about people are dumb or do not care, but when the issue is a personal, internal struggle, people cannot be blamed for missing the signs.

The hardest thing that a person can do when the water is to the neck and rising may be to confide with somebody else that they are struggling. Sharing becomes a point of personal conflict. We question. What will they think of me? If I tell them that I am struggling, will I be judged?

We all possess a default response to the question, "How are you today?" "Oh, I'm OK." "That's good." Look, the question is often rhetorical, a civil and non-threatening question when the response is as per the rules of engagement. Why do we play these silly, inane games? Do you really want to know how I am feeling or are you just trying to be nice and asking only to satisfy your part of the game? Later, when word finally gets out that you have been struggling, the typical response is that "I did ask them how they were, and they said that they were OK." The social niceties of conversation become the biggest enemy for someone who is broken-hearted. Maybe we need to contemplate and rewrite the greeting game and learn to only ask the "How are you going?" question when we are genuinely enquiring and not to flip it off.

CHAPTER 16

LOSS OF TRUST

When the waters are to the neck and rising, there may be loss of trust.

> "But instead, they give me poison for food; they offer me sour wine to satisfy my thirst"

(PSALM 69:21)

A loss of trust can quite naturally follow brokenness. When a heart has been broken for whatever reason, or there is an element of broken-ness evident in an individual, then the ability to extend trust is more than likely compromised from the experience. Trust is hard to redeem once it is lost. We begin to feel that people are intent on playing games at our expense. Pranks and practical jokes become the order of the day. We have become the subject, the target. We desire for people to extend care and we are on the receiving end of poisonous attacks and sourness.

David's heart was crying out for support and care, and instead he was confronted by that which he least deserved or required. It appears that there was a total lack of respect or sensitivity to David's plight and this was outworked, as David described, through poison for food and sour wine for his thirst.

We understand that this passage is fulfilled in a prophetic sense at the crucifixion of Christ. Jesus cried out for something to quench His thirst and was given a sponge soaked in hyssop, with the gospel writers alluding back to this passage of Scripture. It certainly has that connection and application. John Wesley said of the vinegar that these things were metaphorically fulfilled in David, but properly in Christ, the description of whose sufferings was principally intended here by the Holy Ghost.

Expectations and outcomes are at different ends of the continuum. What we see here is a distinct disconnect between the cry of the human heart and the response of supposed "friends." The difficulty comes to light most poignantly as we read. How can someone trust someone when their apparent intent is to further exacerbate the feelings of insecurity and aloneness?

Past hurts generally dictate how we respond to present-day situations. We tend to go into a self-preservation mode that will insulate us from the feelings and emotions that bring us the most pain. Commonly, we will "default" to a tried and perfected response mechanism that will isolate and control our responses and deflect away the greatest impact on us.

David was conscious of his need for support and comfort from his friends, craved it, from what we have read in the preceding verses, "but instead" as the text goes, they were intent on inflicting harm and pain. His expectations were seemingly not met with a correct and appropriate response. The response that David received was an attack on his person. His cry was so heartfelt and personal, but instead he received that which he least deserved. When this occurs, it can appear like a betrayal. Betrayal may be the incorrect response, but with how he was treated, it would be understandable if that was his feeling.

Instead of seriousness, there may be practical jokes. Rather than care, there is neglect. This does not engender confidence in those friends, and as a consequence trust is broken.

When trust has been broken or abused, it can be extremely painful to surrender one's emotional state to the scrutiny of others. At times, we do not fully understand the impact that trust plays in relationships until it has been broken. The consequences of broken trust can play out like an Elizabethan play or a Greek tragedy; it doesn't get any better in the short term. Trust is so easily broken into small pieces and is oh so difficult to restore to its original state. Regaining trust is a very slow and painful process. Our hurts can prevent us from moving on. We would rather withdraw all contact and thereby avoid the potential for additional damage being done to our spirits. Now understand what I am saying at this point. I am not proposing that you try to reconnect with your protagonist; that is not it at all. When there is deep personal hurt, there may be an ignorance of the impact of the taunts or jibes. Besides, they were all in fun anyway—that is the usual response. See, that is the point when someone has broken your trust or affected you in such a way that you are deeply hurt; the one who has perpetrated the offence is oblivious to its impact.

Our thinking becomes clouded in such a way that we begin to think that we will never place ourselves to be vulnerable to another because of those past hurts. Our belief pattern becomes distorted to such an extent that there is no biblical basis to it. We make inner vows.

Vows that are of a negative nature and designed to be our mechanism of personal protection, and as a consequence we isolate ourselves.

Earlier in the chapter, I said, "Trust is hard to redeem once it is lost." I said hard, but not impossible, for in Christ all things are possible to them who believe.

John Wesley wrote that instead of the comfort, which David's condition required his tormentors, it added to his afflictions. When there is a loss of trust, the potential is evident that not only will you continue in your suffering, but that those sufferings will somehow become graver.

What Causes People to Lose Trust?

Trust is one of the primary foundation stones of any relationship. Without trust there can be no relationship. There is an unwillingness to open up oneself to another when there is no trust. Trust may be broken in a number of ways: a confidence broken, inconsistency, physical harm and emotional or psychological abuse. Over time, if there is a loss of trust in a relationship, it is inevitable that at some point in the future there will be a total disintegration and rift.

Taking John Wesley's example, David could not trust people to provide him with something that would meet him at his point of need, but actually exacerbated the situation further.

CHAPTER 17

VENGEFUL

When the waters are to the neck and rising, you may want to seek vengeance and retribution.

"Let the bountiful table set before them become a snare and their prosperity become a trap. Let their eyes go blind so they cannot see, and make their bodies shake continually. Pour out your fury on them; consume them with your burning anger.

Let their homes become desolate and their tents be deserted. To the one you have punished, they add insult to injury; they add to the pain of those you have hurt.

Pile their sins up high, and don't let them go free. Erase their names from the Book of Life; don't let them be counted among the righteous"

(PSALM 69:22–28)

It is interesting to note that it was not what David wanted to personally do to his detractors, but what he wanted God to have done on his behalf. David wanted so much to see those who had unfairly dealt with him to experience the wrath of God.

You want God to champion your cause, to take out those who may be the cause of your anxiety or have added to your misery in life. God may be seen as your knight in shining armour, your masked avenger, the assassin or your defender. You want someone standing beside you, the bigger brother who is going to thrash those who have figuratively beaten you up and stolen your lunch money.

The venom at which David was asking God to deal with those who taunted him appears equivalent to what he himself had received. He wanted it heaped back upon them and then some more. He didn't hold back, either, as you can see. He was very descriptive in how he would like God to deal with those people who did all those things to him. He wanted the comfortable to be made uncomfortable. He wanted to see those who had security to be insecure, and those who had many possessions to experience severe poverty. David was pulling no punches here; he was very sincere in his wishes. He did not want God to leave one aspect of their lives untouched.

David's sense of vengefulness is seen on three levels. It is (1) attacking their lifestyle, (2) attacking their physical health and (3) attacking them at a spiritual level. In actuality, he wanted God to obliterate them, leaving them with absolutely nothing.

Firstly, with lifestyle, David wanted God to deal with his detractors by the statements:

- Let the table set before them become a snare
- Let their security become a trap
- May their homes become desolate
- Their tents be deserted

David wanted to see his tormentors affected in their very place of security. Personal wealth that could bring about a sense of self-satisfaction and achievement, decimated. He used the words "desolate" and "deserted," meaning that all life had been sucked out of them; they were no longer of any use to anyone.

Secondly, at the physical level:

- Let their eyes go blind
- Let their bodies grow weaker and weaker

David wanted to deprive them of their vigour and ability to view life. To lose basic functions such as sight which we take so much for granted and the strength of one's body progressively degenerating.

Thirdly, at the spiritual level:

- Pile their sins up high
- Don't let them go free
- Erase their names from the Book of Life
- Don't let them be counted among the righteous
- Pour out your fury on them
- Consume them with your burning anger

Throughout the Old Testament, we continually see where the people of God have cried out to God for deliverance and vindication. The pattern is clearly defined and repeated throughout. We see it through the books that share the history of His people, throughout the Psalms and also the books of the prophets.

The prophecies of Isaiah, Jeremiah and Ezekiel speak of judgement and total annihilation in some of their dealings with Israel.

Isaiah 51:19–21 – desolation and destruction
Jeremiah 42:17–19 – war, famine and disease
Ezekiel 7:7–9 – destruction, anguish

David saw God as his righteous judge, who would rule in his favour and, as a result, would destroy his enemies. As a consequence, David's enemies would be utterly destroyed, indeed having their names erased forever.

> "For you have judged in my favour, from your throne you have judged with fairness. You have rebuked the nations and destroyed the wicked; you have erased their names forever. The enemy is finished, in endless ruins; the cities you uprooted are now forgotten"
>
> (PSALM 9:4–6)

There may even arise within us this same need and desire to have God avert His ear to our plight and champion our cause, to show His favour to us in this way. As we have seen, the Old Testament is full of instances where either God's wrath has been brought to bear upon the accusers or prayers have gone up crying out for God to intervene. However, there is a better way. Rather than seeking vengeance from God, we need to extend forgiveness. The New Testament provides us with an alternative through the teachings of Jesus. But He goes much further than just forgiving.

Why should I extend forgiveness? The answer to that question lies in the ministry and teachings of Jesus.

Jesus' Message of Forgiveness

Contrast this with the teachings of Jesus.

"If you forgive those who sin against you, your heavenly Father will forgive you. But if you refuse to forgive others, your Father will not forgive your sins"

(MATTHEW 6:14–15)

"Forgive others, and you will be forgiven"

(LUKE 6:37C)

"Father, forgive them, for they don't know what they are doing"

(LUKE 23:34)

When the water is to the neck and rising, forgiveness will be difficult. I know for a fact that extending forgiveness does not come naturally. It can be quite easy to attribute blame, rightly or wrongly, upon others, but this does not necessarily make it right. The need to extend grace and forgiveness is never easy. In the circumstances as outlined throughout this book, where the emotions are stretched and strained, and the emotions have been subject to severe onslaught, forgiveness will not come easily.

There needs to be a willingness on our part to forgive. It is a deliberate act of will to extend forgiveness to someone else. Although God commands forgiveness, there is also within us the capacity to choose to forgive. Our free will, the most valued aspect that differentiates us from the rest of creation, needs to be brought in line with the Word of God and for us to extend forgiveness to those who have offended us.

Results of Unforgiveness

When we read the Bible, we see passages that speak of unforgiveness. A study was conducted by the Centre of Health Care Evaluation which has affiliations with the US Department of Veteran Affairs, Stanford University and the US Health Care System. In the study, Harris and Thoresen devoted a chapter to the topic "Forgiveness, Unforgiveness, Health and Disease" in *The Handbook of Unforgiveness*. In their writings, they explored particular theories that relate to unforgiveness. They concluded the following: "Evidence has been produced linking both forgiveness and unforgiveness to short-term physiological variables, such as cortisol reactivity (Berry & Worthington, 2001), blood pressure, and skin conductance (Lawler et al., 2003; Witvliet, Ludwig, & Vander Laan, 2001). Coupled with the related literature on stress and health, this evidence makes hypotheses directly linking unforgiveness and forgiveness with health and disease variables more plausible and ripe to be tested." Cortisol is a hormone released by the cortex (outer portion) of the adrenal gland when a person is under stress. Cortisol levels are now considered a biological marker of suicide risk.[11]

They viewed unforgiveness as a chronic stress response because of the similar nature of health problems associated with each. Harris and Thoresen continued to speak of unforgiveness leading to behaviours that may cause health problems.

"At least two processes might implicate unforgiveness in the erosion of social networks and support. First, the unforgiving person, who may be angry, hostile, ruminating, and attached to his or her victim role, may have friends and acquaintances who tire of attending

[11] *The Gale Encyclopedia of Medicine.* Copyright 2008 The Gale Group, Inc. All rights reserved.

to the person's misery. Second, the dispositionally unforgiving person, untrusting of people and fearful of re-victimization, may avoid social contact or may limit the extent to which he or she allows himself or herself to be vulnerable in relationships. If unforgiveness reduces social contact, support, and integration by these or other mechanisms, the health benefits of these contacts will be lost. It is also important to note that not all social contact is health promoting. In some cases, the anger or fear associated with unforgiveness might motivate healthy changes or reductions in unhealthy social contact."

Although the study associated with the published document presented by Harris and Thoresen was founded upon hypothesis and theoretical models, there appears to be a clear indication that a direct correlation exists between forgiveness/unforgiveness and health and disease. To see that science is actually exploring these concepts provides us with some insight into the thinking that does exist in the clinical environment and to the level of credence that is placed on the impact of unforgiveness in an individual's own body. Science and clinical studies look as though they are conforming to the biblical view, and this is encouraging. It would be another thing if science admitted to that.

The study expressed unforgiveness as a product of rumination or extended pondering on an issue. In other words, the person gets stuck in a place of negative emotions and, as a result, has an inability to move forward from that emotional state of flux. This is a place that is far removed from the immediate response to a perceived injustice. The result of this form of unforgiveness can see an increase in unsafe coping mechanisms, for example, substance abuse and avoidance.

Unforgiveness can ultimately give way to bitterness, and then you could say that the person is really bogged down and entering an emotional wilderness. Bitterness can be seen as the result of a persistent emotional imbalance.

What is forgiveness? The following is a definition that can be found in the *Man to Man Manual* and, I think, really encapsulates the meaning of forgiveness.

Forgiveness is: "when love accepts deliberately the hurts and abrasions of life and drops all the charges against the other person. We recognise that life is not always fair, and we lay aside the right and the need to seek revenge."[12]

In essence, this means that the right to attribute blame is forfeited as a deliberate act. The decision to forgive is a choice we make deliberately.

Benefits of Forgiveness

If, in psychological theory, there are negative health impacts as a result of unforgiveness, then it is plausible to conclude that better health results from a forgiving heart.

An article authored by Elizabeth Scott, M.S. on the "Benefits of Forgiveness" discussed a study in the *Journal of Behavioral Medicine* that found forgiveness was good for the heart, literally. Forgiveness was associated with lower heart rate and blood pressure, as well as a stress relief. She continued that forgiveness was positively associated with five measures of health: physical symptoms, medication used, sleep quality, fatigue and somatic complaints. Forgiveness brings a reduction in depression symptoms, strengthened spirituality.

Stress has physical outcomes, including on our body, our mood and our emotions. It is these stress factors that can also have an effect on our willingness to forgive.

---

[12] Man to Man Manual © 2005 Careforce Ministries Limited, pp. 10–5

It is true that forgiveness is better for the forgiver than for the one who has been forgiven. Why? Well, look back at the previous paragraph and you have your answer. If the release that is provided through the reduction in your stress levels and impacts your heart rate and blood pressure because of having extended forgiveness, then forgiveness is not optional but mandatory from a healthy lifestyle perspective. This does not necessarily mean you have to speak directly with the person with whom you hold unforgiveness towards; they may be ignorant of having offended you or be aware of the impact they have had on you in a negative sense.

The other area which benefits from us extending forgiveness is in the spiritual. Our spiritual health is enhanced. Forgiveness is obedience to God. Forgiveness is part of the character of God as seen through the cross of Christ.

Scriptures also provide us with the pattern for forgiveness. Repentance is clearly linked to forgiveness; restoration of relationship is the ultimate endgame of forgiveness. A failure on the part of the offender does not release the offended party from an obligation to forgive. Forgiveness is about a heart attitude. If you cannot forgive someone from your heart, then you still have a way to go to have truly and fully forgiven. Remember, forgiveness is more a lifestyle than a definitive one-off event. You may forgive someone intellectually, but your heart is not in it, but over time, as you extend God's blessing to the other party, then a transformation will occur in your heart that brings it into union with the original intellectual action.

We release our heart from the bile of unforgiveness and its potential for us to become bitter and twisted. Forgiveness is more about us and not the other person. To release our hearts and minds from the oppression and the bondage of unforgiveness activates the goodness of God in our lives. We cannot honour God and carry unforgiveness in our hearts. By doing so, we place a limit on what God can do in and through us. Our hearts cannot be divided and compartmentalised in such a manner.

> "Therefore if you bring your gift to the altar, and remember that your brother has something against you, leave your gift there at the altar, and go your way. First be reconciled to your brother, and then come and offer your gift"
>
> (Matthew 5:23–24, NKJV)

Acceptance of our offerings is contingent upon our relationships and our heart towards others. Jesus said that it is better to leave the offering, seek restoration and then come again and finalise the transaction. The pattern is established and not confined to the cultural act of sacrifice in ancient times but extends to this present day, in that we are to offer ourselves as a living sacrifice. Therefore, before we can truthfully and truly do that act of worship we should consider our relationships and engage in restoration through the offering of forgiveness then offer ourselves to God. But alas, we would rather live in a place of denial and pretend that all is right with our relationships and that the fault is with the other party and "play church." We have received the gift of forgiveness when we did not deserve it, and yet we do not offer to extend grace and forgive others. This is reminiscent of the parable of the unforgiving servant in Matthew 18:21–35. One servant is offered forgiveness from the master when he owes much, then does not extend the same to another who owes him much less.

Now, as I said earlier, there will be times when a face-to-face act of forgiveness will not be appropriate, but the act of forgiveness is. As I have already said, forgiveness is about you and your attitude, not about the other person. When there is a willingness, or rather the decision to choose to forgive, then there is a sense of emotional release.

Tension is released when we forgive. We need to disarm the effects and to dismantle the altar of our hurts and pain. This altar is not a place of sacrifice but more a morbid memorial, a place where we justify our hurt and pain through the unforgiving heart. Burn down the altar. Do it now. Permit yourself to be altered by the forgiveness of God and be released from the tension of event/s that has attempted to dominate your life and your existence.

Forgiveness is a deliberate action. Your whole being is dysfunctional when you live with unforgiveness in your heart. Bring your heart and mind into order again and under the Lordship of Christ. Do not delay.

The Power of Forgiveness

Power is released through forgiveness: power to change, power for restoration of relationship.

A 2004 article released by *Harvard Health* described the benefits that accompanied forgiveness. In summary, they highlighted the following:

- Reduced stress
- Better heart health
- Strong relationships
- Reduced pain
- Greater happiness

To know that our health and well-being are directly correlated with forgiveness, this should then raise within us a convincing argument to choose to forgive. Now consider these medical outcomes with what Jesus said:

> "If you forgive those who sin against you, your heavenly Father will forgive you. But if you refuse to forgive others, your Father will not forgive your sins"
>
> (MATTHEW 6:14–15)

We are at peril of not being forgiven by God if we chose not to forgive another person. A choice to not forgive places me contrary to the Word of God, and therefore the whole health and well-being concept raised by the Harvard article becomes totally irrelevant, as my spiritual future is placed in jeopardy. Consider the importance placed on forgiveness by the statement of Jesus, as found in the gospel of Luke.

> "Judge not [neither pronouncing judgement nor subjecting to censure], and you will not be judged; do not condemn and pronounce guilty, and you will not be condemned and pronounced guilty; acquit and forgive and release (give up resentment, let it drop), and you will be acquitted and forgiven and released"
>
> (LUKE 6:37, AMP)

The final words provide the keys to forgiveness:

- Give up resentment
- Let it drop

Then on that basis, you will then be:

- Acquitted
- Forgiven
- Released

Forgiveness releases each of us from the bondage of unforgiveness and the resentment and bitterness that partner with it. Therefore, in order to see true freedom of the Spirit, I must forgive. It is an imperative not a suggestion or a good idea worthy of consideration.

CHAPTER 18

ACKNOWLEDGEMENT
OF OUR STATE

When the waters are to our neck, we need to acknowledge our present state.

"I am suffering and in pain"

(PSALM 69:29A)

At this point in David's prayer, he began to articulate (verbalise) his suffering and pain. The level of importance and priority that needs to be placed on acknowledging our state, that is, acknowledge our suffering, identifying the source of our pain and vocalising or articulating our pain, cannot be understated. In so doing, we are giving voice to our inner hurts and needs. This, in itself, can be quite a healing experience, but also brings additional risks with it. There is the risk that we will be misunderstood. There is also the risk that we will be judged by others.

By articulating our suffering and pain, I do not mean that we talk with anyone and everyone who crosses our path about our situation, but rather with trusted people who can share our burden and clearly will be able to empathise with us. In that place where the water is to the neck and rising and there has been a loss of trust, another apparent risk is to begin to trust again. Even if loss of trust is a perception or a false truth, then the ability to extend trust will be another whole journey in itself.

Sharing can be so hard to do because of the fear of being judged, to be treated like a person who has some contagious disease. As I have already said, we need to identify where we are emotionally. In order to be able to have the potential to move forward, it is crucial to know where we are—at this present point in time. If we understand life is about journey or pilgrimage, then the fundamental question to ask oneself is: "Where am I?" Once that question is answered, then progress can be made by the next question: "Where am I going?" David identified that he was suffering and in pain.

We need to resolve our own personal state. People, family and friends can tell us, but we tend to not acknowledge or give credence to their statements. It can get to the point where we become dismissive of them and their opinions. We would prefer to live in a perpetual state of denial, or at least in that place where we know the degree of our pain and suffering. There is a strange sense of solace in the known and this same sense does not exist in the unknown. We do not know the pain that we will potentially encounter if we were to contemplate change. Therefore, we remain content with the status quo no matter how harmful that may be to our well-being.

Humility Is Required

This may come across to you, the reader, as a little strange, that we need to be humble. The dictionary definition for the word humble describes it this way: "having or showing a modest or low estimate of one's own importance." Society determines that we should have it all together and trust in our sense of individuality. The problem with that concept is that if we stuff it up, where do we go from there? Humility dictates that we need to lower our own perception of self-importance.

Jesus explained this aspect in what we term the Sermon on the Mount.

"Blessed are the poor in spirit"

(PSALM 5:3)

Who are the poor in spirit? The poor in spirit are people who realise and acknowledge their need for God. What does this have to do with where I am at? My answer to that question: it has everything to do with it! While we are in the waters of despair with the constant threat of being overwhelmed by them, we need to acknowledge that we cannot do it on our own. We do not have the capacity to fight against such sheer volume. If we stop struggling, the inevitable will occur and we will go under. We do not find safety there. We do require outside intervention. In the Australian context, it would be like being at the beach and being caught in a rip and requiring a lifesaver (lifeguard) to come to our aid and bring us into the safety of the shore. Outside help requires invitation: "Hey, over here. Help me out! I can't do this on my own. I've tried, and if anything, it is getting worse." Invitation can only occur after we acknowledge that we cannot do it on our own or in our own strength. David's cry was for someone to come beside him (verse

20) and to show him comfort, but he was not yet in that position to ask until he could acknowledge his pain. The intent and thought was there in his desire, but he was not yet ready until he acknowledged his need.

A common myth is that having to ask for help is a sign of weakness. By asking, you are giving a friend the privilege of helping you. Our minds can be so messed up, and as a consequence we are unable to make even simple decisions or to undertake the process of pros and cons required in problem solving. Jesus says that God blesses those who reach the conclusion of "I can't do this on my own." In response, the poor in spirit are given the Kingdom of Heaven. To learn this powerful truth can be very liberating. The first time you share can feel awkward, but each time you do you are claiming back lost ground. I know the feeling of sharing that first time. It isn't easy. Your mouth is dry, your stomach is in knots and your pulse is racing. You are fighting against the fear of getting the story wrong, but it is not so much about the story in itself but about the feelings and emotions that are raging inside you.

Our thinking becomes distorted as a result of our suffering and pain. If I tell them what I am going through, they may not like me. They may even walk away from me. They may judge me. Your silence can become the barrier you hide behind, your "safe refuge." Emotionally you have retreated into your castle, raised the drawbridge and are peering out from the comparative safety of the parapet. As twisted as your thinking may be at this time, there may even be an element of pride.

Change cannot be effected until we resolve within ourselves that there is in fact an issue or problem that needs to be dealt with. The statement that David made in this verse is the turning point in the whole Psalm, the lynchpin that begins the process of change. I use the word begins because this statement is not the end result with the answer in a miraculous intervention by God. This is not God riding in on a white steed with sword drawn, slaying all the dragons that are oppressing us then sweeping us up and whisking us off to a place of safe refuge. The saying goes that every journey begins with the first step. The statement "I am suffering and in pain" is the first step in the journey of recovery. If we do not acknowledge our state, then we are in denial. Denial is not a good place. Denial draws us into untruth. Denial sucks hope from us. Denial denies us the opportunity for inner healing. Only truth can draw us out of the place where the water is to the neck and rising, and into a place of safety.

Until we reach that point where we can look ourselves in the mirror and truthfully acknowledge that, yes, there is a problem, we will continue to be buffeted with all the cares of life and become more and more overwhelmed with whatever it is that has put us there in the first place. We need to become emotionally honest with how we are feeling. Emotional honesty is not a negative concept. It does not cut across the truth of God's Word. God wants us to honestly express how we are feeling. When I am weak then You are strong, that is what the Word of God says. It is in my weakness and vulnerability that You reveal Yourself to me and transform my life.

The idea that this gives me is that this is about profession, not confession. Confession implies that you are guilty or in the wrong and that which you have been accused is true. Profession is about declaration. It is declaring openly, voluntarily and fully. By implication profession is yielding or a change in one's conviction.[13] David was making a profession of fact; a faith profession.

Change begins to take place during this time. Firstly, it is a change in attitude, not necessarily in situation. It was in the midst of the

---

[13] J. H. Thayer, *Greek-English Lexicon*, 1981

floodwaters of life that David began his transformation. David was humble enough in his heartfelt need to be able to voice his heart and to acknowledge his need. This is healthy. Here was David, in a state of emotional dysfunction, and he was able to finally come to the point of saying to God, "I'm hurting here." True transformation can only begin at the low point, when we are at our lowest. Why? Because it is at that low point where we have run out of our own answers and excuses and frankly we cannot go any lower. All of our theories have been tested and found wanting and we do not know where to turn. Now this is not a quick three-step programme where we do this and that will happen, and then everything will be all right. I know in my own situation it was not until I came to the point of saying this is too hard and I cannot do it on my own that healing could begin to come. As I write this, I know that I am still susceptible to the feelings of becoming overwhelmed, but the difference is that I can now identify some of the triggers to my emotional state and hopefully make appropriate steps to manage my thoughts and feelings. This is a much better place to be, but it has not come easily. Until I came to the realisation that, yes, I was suffering and in pain, I was neither willing nor equipped to begin the dialogue that needed to occur.

Now this journey is not without its pain and there are no quick fixes. It takes a lot of hard work. That is, unless God turns up and performs a miracle of transformation, but that is the exception and not the rule. I believe in miracles, do not get me wrong. But can you imagine the impact such an instantaneous transformation would have on someone's life? Someone who has built up a lifetime of habits and has also established unhealthy coping mechanisms. I believe that God is a God of order and structure, so as a result the re-engineering process is one that is enshrined in time. That is time to heal.

You just need to look at creation to see how ordered and structured His beautiful handiwork is and come to the realisation that where there has been disorder and dysfunction, He (God) will provide a safe place for healing and transformation. Therefore, the process of transformation allows for a change of mindset, the ability to process our "junk" and adopt healthy practices. Change is individual and will vary for each person. This process obviously may require outside influence, either professionally by a counsellor/psychologist or personally from a trusted friend. This further engages us with our thought processes and brings about a level of accountability but not abdication of ownership of the situation in our transformation.

My Personal Experience

Even during the course of writing this book, I have had a poignant reminder of the dangers of suppression. At that time, I felt personally aggrieved and, over the course of a couple of days, played through various scenarios that were my imagined discussions. By internalising, I found my emotions flatlining while, conversely, anger rose from deep within me. My only response to my wife Jenny was, "I feel flat." I felt rejected, I felt judged and my sense of worth and value were in the toilet. Once the opportunity to express my feelings and opinions eventuated, it was as if that acid of anger and the bile of bitterness were released. Now this did not occur in an unhealthy way, but through it all I was able to maintain my dignity. The acid of bad feelings, emotions that were so real in the pit of my stomach, dissipated in that moment. Together with that, the tension in my facial muscles was released. To me this was so tangible, yet to some extent it was also difficult to explain. However, if I had not dealt with it when the opportunity arose, and in the manner I did at that moment, then there was the potential for that anger and bitterness to ferment some more and then spew forth in a tirade that would be extremely hurtful.

What I learned from my experience were these few things. There are positives and negatives:

Negative side

- Do not try to work it out in your own mind.
- Do not play out how you think the conversation should go.
- Do not try to "produce an imagined end result."

Positive side

- Only communicate in a healthy manner.
- Speak of feelings.
- Do not attribute blame.
- Release and freedom only come through disclosure, that is, speaking it out, bringing that which is in the dark into the light.

For a moment, I want to expand slightly on both lists. In a place of emotional confusion, it is very easy to magnify a situation beyond its true extent. So in this state, if we try to work things out in our mind, we are working with flawed information, some of it may even well be based on fact, but fact which has been distorted to such an extent that it no longer resembles the original. That is why it is so important to have an external party to assist with the process, as they are objective in their observations and are not caught in the moment as it were. As you can see by the list on the positive side, the main ingredient revolves exclusively around communication. It is how we communicate that is important; we need to be true to ourselves. Why have I also added: not to attribute blame. The blame game is counterproductive in the healing process. Blaming allows us to deflect attention from ourselves and thereby provides us with a mechanism where we can "justify" our sense of indignation, further hampering the healing process.

Blaming is the seedbed of unforgiveness. Unforgiveness breeds bitterness which in turn leads to, for the sake of better words, alienation and strife. If we truthfully and honestly speak from a place of humility, then a change will begin to occur within us. *The Message* version states:

> "I'm hurt and in pain; give me space for healing, and mountain air"
>
> (PSALM 69:29, *THE MESSAGE*)

It is true we do need some space to heal and the freshness and crispness of pure mountain air, which speaks of the presence of God, to clear out the stale stench of our lives.

Truly, I feel blessed with the people who have come around me and who have supported me. Also, the love of a faithful wife has been an undergirding for me and an invaluable support, as she has seen me behind the closed doors. Now the opportunity I experienced may not necessarily be the case in every situation, but speaking out in a healthy manner does bring healing.

Our words can also trip us up. The Bible says that from out of the heart the mouth speaks, and that is never truer than during this experience. If my heart had been full of bitterness and deceit, then maybe the words that would have been spoken would have been quite different, and therefore the outcome. The feeling in the pit of my stomach felt so real. The physical symptoms were clearly distinguishable and describable. I also found that it was not necessary to say everything that was experienced or thought. If I had conveyed what I really thought or felt, I would have brought disrepute to God and myself and I would have wounded more harshly than I had been in the first instance. The experience, although painful, has reminded me there is a right way to handle conflict. The right way is a godly way. I was then able to walk away with personal integrity intact, at peace and free.

Let me encourage you to learn the skills in order to be able to communicate in a healthy manner. I know how easy it is to lash out, but this only destroys relationships and serves to remind us that we need to be careful in what we say. The power of our words to either lift up or to cut down is such a potent phenomenon. As much as we have seen how words can affect us, we need to remember that our words can have the same effect on those with whom we communicate. We can quickly escalate a situation and make it unredeemable. That is not a great outcome for anyone and especially not for a Christian.

Men, you need to learn to communicate your feelings. Do not continue to suffer in silence. Do not continue to put your family and friends through any more torment because of your stubbornness. Do not let your pride hinder you from experiencing all that God has to offer you. You are short-changing yourself. I understand the arguments. I have either heard them or used them myself. I have tried silence. I have tried denial. I have tried anger as a mechanism to push people away. Good-intentioned people who had my well-being in mind. They expressed great concern for me, and yet I pushed them away with my attitude. Guys, do not push away people who love you. Learn to talk about where you are at. Speaking about where you are emotionally is like a release valve on a pressure cooker; it lets off some of the steam.

As I said earlier there are risks, but when you risk in a healthy manner the benefits far outweigh the cost.

"Rescue me, O God, by your saving power"

(PSALM 69:29B)

Some translations read, "Set me on high" and this draws a different thought or concept to our understanding of what David was trying to voice through his pray rather than rescue me.

What does it mean to be "set on high"? David was in the depths of despair, feeling overwhelmed as if he was in a flooded river, and understandably he wanted out of his situation. He was praying for God to lift him out of his despair to a place of safety and security. On high typifies a lofty place such as an eagle's eyrie (nest). On high is a place of sanctuary, free from predators and natural forces. The need to be in a place of safety that is far removed from the circumstances of life, where the pain and suffering is so acute, is genuine. This is conveyed in *The Message* version with the phrase "mountain air."

When the cause of our suffering is akin to water to the neck; a place far removed from it is desirable. God, I would much rather be in a high place, safe and dry, than fighting the tides of life where I may lose my life in the process.

In Psalm 61, David talked about having God to lead him to the "towering rock of safety." There he found a safe refuge and a fortress where his enemies cannot reach him. Rescue is in God's economy. He has ransomed us through His Son. The ultimate exchange has occurred through Christ dying on the cross instead of me being subject to the judgement of my sinful nature and personal actions. The wonder of the Grace of God cannot be understated. His heart has always been about relationship, and the rescue brought about through Jesus Christ sees us begin to walk in a life of liberty and freedom unlike anything that we have ever experienced before. God desires each of us to be in a place of safety and living a life of victory. Being in a citadel, where we can live in peace and be refreshed. To know our God can bring restoration to our lives and to see Him desiring to reconnect in relationship.

The picture of the eagle's nest set on high on a mountain peak, far above all peril and predators, gives us an insight into the plans of God for each of us. His heart is toward each of us; He does not turn away from His children.

This concept of sanctuary is a true replication of safety to each of us. In our own strength we try to create this through our coping mechanisms, but they are only like the bed of the stream which is full of mire and offers us no foothold. They are momentary and then we are back in the place of our torment.

> "He lifted me out of the slimy pit, out of the mud and mire; he
> set my feet on a rock and gave me a firm place to stand"
>
> (PSALM 40:2)

Rock speaks of stability and a sure foundation. To understand that God can translate us from a place of uncertainty and insecurity, the miry pit as it were, and lifts us up to a higher place is comforting.

> "He drew me up out of a horrible pit [a pit of tumult and of
> destruction], out of the miry clay (froth and slime), and set
> my feet upon a rock, steadying my steps and establishing my
> goings"
>
> (PSALM 40:2, AMP)

God is establishing my ways and setting my paths, giving me clear direction. A life that was full of tumult and destructive is made sure. When God does something incredible in our lives, we see that our lives are turned around and the turmoil is replaced by peace, and destruction is replaced with restoration.

CHAPTER 19

PRAISE AND THANKSGIVING

When the water is to the neck and rising, **we need to** offer praise and thanksgiving to God.

This is not about a want to praise God, but a conscious and deliberate act of our will to offer to our Creator our voice in praise and worship to Him. Sometimes we get to the point of identifying our need, but we get stuck in that place; there is a natural progression at work here. We need to move past the point of acknowledging our state and begin to offer praise to God. This is more about us and less about God, that ability to lift our eyes off our circumstances and focus on Him.

> "Then I will praise God's name with singing, and I will honour Him with thanksgiving. For this will please the LORD more than sacrificing cattle, more than presenting a bull with its horns and hooves"
>
> (PSALM 69:30–31)

I am not being trite at this point. When we are experiencing such negative feelings as have been discussed thus far, praise can be the last thing we want to do. As a Christian, I recognise that praise is difficult at times. But when we have recognised that we are suffering and in pain that is either physical or emotional, to offer praise to a God we feel has forgotten us seems rather odd. To demonstrate such a strong exercise of our will while in a place of suffering tends to go against all logic. At this point logic has gone out the door, along with some of our perceptions and self-views. This in itself is another "illogical" action.

Even though David was going through all this anguish as outlined throughout his prayer, he still took time to devote praise to God. He had determined that God is worthy of praise. He made a choice to praise God. This was a deliberate act of his will. David knew the power and potency of praising God. Previous experience reminded David of the benefits of offering praise to God. Throughout the Psalms, David constantly reminded himself of the goodness of God and, as a direct result, offered his praise and thanksgiving. Even in this psalm he had made that very comment. He said that God's lovingkindness, that is His unfailing love, is good. David went so far as to write in Psalm 63:3:

"Because Your lovingkindness is better than life."

This may be one of the hardest aspects to do. The last thing that you want to do when the water is to the neck and rising is to offer up praise and thanksgiving. You are in the middle of this raging emotional torrent, you feel overwhelmed and all of your strength is devoted solely to survival mode, but David said the key lies in praising God. Yes, praise can be inconvenient. You may say, "But I don't feel like it." "What do I have to be thankful for?" You miss the point.

Praise lifts our eyes and attention off our circumstances; it doesn't change them. This isn't some form of diversion therapy. Regardless of whether this is water to the neck and rising, either real or metaphorical, our "rescue" can only be accomplished by moving our vision off our circumstances and into the source of our recovery. A person cannot be rescued from a flooded stream or clinging for life on a cliff face until such time as he has cast his eyes towards the rescuer with the lifeline.

David's decision was to praise his God. Even in his emptiness and dryness, he deliberately purposed to praise his God. He saw praise of greater value than the sacrifice of prized livestock. David did not offer what he had in the form of material possession, but rather he gave out what he did not have. He offered himself to God as an instrument of praise. Despite not hearing from God or having any apparent God-consciousness, he praised from a point of emptiness. David was driven to this point of sacrifice because he had nowhere else to go. This is not about getting, but about giving. David's perspective was dramatically changed at this point. He was still in the waters up to his neck, that hadn't changed, yet this led to a remarkable revelation while in those waters of despair.

Revelation can come in the dry times and it is like water to a dry and thirsty land. It can come in the times when we feel so far from God that we even begin to think, "Is God even interested in me?" We will soak it up. It is food to our souls. But that type of revelation can only come when we deliberately purpose to offer a sacrifice of praise to God. If our lives are at saturation level, then the impact can mirror soil that has been rained upon for days and it cannot be contained anymore, and it begins to run off and is lost. This does show us that God is indeed interested in us and will provide us with revelation of His nature and His goodness. We would normally associate hearing the voice of God when times are good and our devotion and relationship are travelling well, but we should not assume that this is always the case. It is in our state of emptiness that God brings about such a revelation of Himself and His nature, that there is an encounter with Him like no other. It is these encounters that have life-changing impact. The emptiness of the heart is filled. The dryness of the spirit is replaced with vitality and freshness of life. A vessel can only be filled when it is empty. Kingdom principles are contrary to human reasoning; the first shall be last, wisdom out of foolishness, reaping and sowing, something out of nothing. This contrarian approach that God provides as part of His order reveals to us His true majestic splendour and defies human logic in being able to explain away what occurs in our lives.

Nowhere in this Psalm did David say that God either answered him or indeed rescued him from his plight. We all have stories where we have been through an experience and have either not received an answer from God or been rescued from out of our circumstances.

What Does Praising God Do to Our Spirit?

Praising God **lifts our spirits**. Have you ever noticed that when you are feeling low and you go to church and start to sing the songs that there is a change in attitude? You are momentarily moved from your state of flatness and you begin to feel better on the inside, even if it is only momentarily.

Praise is an elixir, not of the snake-oil-seller variety but a tangible lifter of our spirits. David wrote of a merry heart:

"A merry heart does good, like a medicine"

(PROVERBS 17:22, NKJV)

136

"But a broken spirit saps a person's strength"

(PROVERBS 17:22, NLT)

Praise does make us feel happy, and therefore if our heart is happy then our spirit has been fed and has derived strength and nourishment, and as a consequence we feel good.

Praise should be in every part of me.

"Let all that I am praise the LORD; May I never forget the good things he does for me"

(PSALM 103:2)

The NKJV puts it this way:

"Bless the Lord, O my soul, and forget not all His benefits..."

God's benefits are as follows:

- He forgives our sins.
- God heals all our diseases.
- He redeems our life from destruction.
- He crowns us with lovingkindness and tender mercies.
- He fills my life with good things.
- He renews our youth like the eagle's.

The passage also outlines other positives of a life in God:

- He gives righteousness and justice to all who are unfairly treated.
- God is compassionate and merciful.

- He is slow to get angry and filled with unfailing love.
- God will not constantly accuse us.
- He does not deal harshly with us, as we deserve.
- God's unfailing love is as great as the height of the heavens.
- He removes our sins as far from us as the east is from the west.
- God is like a father to his children, tender and compassionate.
- His love will remain forever.

"I said to the LORD, 'You are my Master! Every good thing I have comes from you'"

(PSALM 16:2)

"Let all that I am praise the LORD"

(PSALM 104:1)

"Why am I discouraged? Why is my heart so sad? I will put my hope in God! I will praise him again – my Saviour and my God!"

(PSALM 42:5)

"I look for your help, O Sovereign LORD. You are my refuge…"

(PSALM 141:8)

Praising God **is good**.

"I will sacrifice a voluntary offering to you; I will prise your name, O LORD, for it is good"

(PSALM 54:6)

On this particular occasion, he was able to bear testimony that God had indeed rescued him from his troubles. Praise is a way of thanking God for His goodness towards us.

Praising God **is appropriate**. Praising God is necessary and should never only be associated with the good things. If we only praised God in the good times, where is the sacrifice in that? Our praises would become shallow, riddled with relief, assumption and presumption. Come to think of it, would we even praise God? Would we become blasé because of the constant answering of prayer?

Praising God can be **a sacrifice**. Sacrifice implies a cost and praising God costs us. In praise we are giving of ourselves to God out of our self. The cost is seen in taking the time and may even be an imposition on our sensibilities. When the water is to the neck and rising, we may be offering praise "on credit," as we feel we have nothing to offer Him. But the cost should not be calculated in financial terms. Our greatest "gift" to God is to submit ourselves and give out of lack, and then we will begin to see extraordinary things occur. It is praise that is offered out of emptiness. This praise should not be seen or considered as a last-ditched effort either to sway or manipulate God into acting on our behalf and in our favour. It is only out of our emptiness that we can be filled. It is only out of emptiness that we can see the God of our Salvation do the work that could not otherwise be evident in our "fullness."

Praising God **is an act of my will**. Praise is a deliberate act and not done by way of accident, out of obligation or compunction. "I will bless the Lord at all times, his praise shall continually be in my mouth"[14] reflects an act of our will. We are not compelled to praise God, but rather we determine in our hearts to offer praise to Him. Praise is a

---

[14] Psalm 34:1, KJV

deliberate choice that we **need** to make. Maybe we should consider that "I will praise" is actually "I choose to praise." We need praise in our lives.

Isn't it interesting that there is a "sometimes"? There are some times when God hears and rescues us, and there are some times when He doesn't. What is it about God and this sometimes? We need to submit to the Sovereignty of God and His goodness. We do not know His plans for us. As painful as it is to go through those periods, these can be times of extraordinary opportunity for God to work in our lives. The results may leave us battered and bruised, and we carry the scars from those periods as a constant reminder. We need to submit to God's goodness. Apostle Paul wrote:

> "Giving thanks always for all things to God the Father in the name of our Lord Jesus Christ"
>
> (EPHESIANS 5:20, NKJV)

> "For we know that all things work together for good to those who love God"
>
> (ROMANS 8:28, NKJV)

To state the obvious, God is God, and we need to come under His Lordship and submit to it. This takes tremendous sacrifice when the waters are to the neck and rising. David was able to do it. It doesn't seem to be an easy thing to do in the first instance, but the benefits of doing so are truly fulfilling.

We need to learn to give praise and thanksgiving. Yes, offer thanksgiving for His faithfulness. David talked of God's unfailing love; recognised it, acknowledged it and thanked Him for it. Began to recall those times when God had shown His favour and faithfulness and praised Him. I can remember as a child hearing sermons from preachers on the subject of praising God when we don't feel like it. The point is to be prepared to praise God because He is worthy of that praise. Learn from David's example. You may travel a similar road as he and will need to reach that same fork in road at some point, and when you do be prepared to come to the same conclusion and praise God.

CHAPTER 20

GOD IS THERE

When the water is to the neck and rising, God is there.

"The humble will see their God at work"

(PSALM 69:32A)

You may think that this would be far from the truth as you read earlier about God having forgotten us. In the depths of his despair, David knew that his God was there. He voiced his concerns and grievances, but now there was a marked change in his attitude and in the style of prayer that he was offering. I will now say this: it is OK to voice our grievances, BUT it is our motivation that will give us away. If our motives involve trying to win the pity vote or to show a facade of false humility, then we should keep our mouth shut. We also need to be careful with whom we talk and also how we talk. There is a need to share our burdens. That need is not to add burden to someone else, but rather to act more as a cathartic experience, where we are releasing the emotional bile. The end result should replicate a healing experience, not a spill-our-guts-now-I-feel-OK session. Instead what we should be doing is bringing into the light of day our innermost thoughts and feelings and potentially seeing a release of burden. Again that is if our motivation is right and we seriously want to be free to live a life of victory and liberty.

Voicing grievances should never be about telling a "woe is me" story to all and sundry. That can quickly become a whinging session and is a sure-fire way to alienate your friends. If the story only becomes the focus of our conversation, then the danger is that the potential for healing is dramatically minimised and change will not result.

David transitioned away from his position in verse 17: "Don't hide from your servant." What has brought about this dramatic change? This is not rocket science; there is a direct correlation with David's determination to offer praise and thanksgiving. Praise lifts the spirit. David did not become resigned to being forever in that place, where his prayer began, but as he determined in his heart to offer praise and thanksgiving, he would not be disappointed. For David to get to this place, his mindset had revolutionarily changed. This is no quick three-step pathway to healing. Healing is a process. As I have already stated, if God wants to perform a miracle, that is his domain and is the exception and not the rule. We need to trust in the sovereignty of God in all of this. God has our best interests at heart even though at times we would question that, but when you consider the thoughts that David went through, then we are in good company. If we try to shortcut the process or short-circuit it, we are in for a great deal of personal pain. Do that at your own peril.

The keys that David identified enabled his change in attitude: he acknowledged his state of emotion; he offered praise to God and was followed by the realisation that God was indeed with him no matter what may come. Revelation comes out of a full heart.

The Promise

There is a distinct promise evident in David's words:

"The humble will see their God at work and be glad"

(PSALM 69:32)

God Is at Work

This promise is direct from God. By inference if the humble see their God at work, then God is there in our circumstance. He is there when the water is to our neck and rising. He is there when our feelings are so fragile and our emotions so raw that we feel that we cannot go on. He is there when we feel alone, alienated and isolated. In that place of aloneness and suffering, there is a message of hope. That is a message that we need to receive when the water is to the neck and rising. In that place there is a feeling of hopelessness, of being without hope, and of having no hope. Our expectations are so low that we begin to believe that is our lot in life and no good thing can be ours to possess. We are in a perpetual state of loss and crisis. When the water is to the neck and rising, we miss out on the inheritance that is ours as a result of being a child of the living God. We do not see our potential in Christ. We feel robbed of the promises of God, as there is no joy and we are rarely in a place of peace. Our constant struggle seems to prevent us from entering in the rest that God has promised.

So who are the humble? The *New International Version* translates this word as "the poor." So then, who are the poor? Are these people who only have no money? Jesus spoke of those who are poor in spirit in what we call the Sermon on the Mount. The *New Living Translation* says:

> "God blesses those who are poor and realize their need for Him"
>
> (MATTHEW 5:3)

We need to come to that point of realising that we do need God and cannot do life in isolation and by ourselves. We need to concede ground, not by giving it up in a negative sense, but at that point of time, whenever that may be, to yield ourselves wholeheartedly to God and His purposes. In so doing, we will see God at work and be glad.

The difficulty is to get to that point of decision while in a place of hopelessness. You can see that there was a distinct process of thought that David went through to be able to reach the point of decision and then to speak so emphatically about what God could do. Joy and gladness are found in the place of God's handiwork.

The Promise Is, We Will Be Glad

The promise is that when we see God at work, we will be glad. When God works in our lives, then there is lifting of our spirit within us and we cannot remain in the place of sadness, but rather we are lifted to the place of gladness. Desperation is replaced with a peace that only God can give.

> "Let all who seek God's help live in joy"
>
> (PSALM 69:32B)

When God Works, the End Result Is Joy and Happiness

Be encouraged that your God is for you, that you are seeing Him at work. Seek Him out. Become proactive during your state of inertia. Take heart and be encouraged. Joy is the reward of those who seek out God. He does not disappoint or disapprove of someone who searches for Him with a sincere heart. Do not wait or be passive and expect that it will all come to you. You are only setting yourself up for disappointment and disillusionment. Begin to take steps in the right direction.

Torment has been replaced with life. When we seek after God, as the *Amplified* says,

"Inquiring for and requiring Him [as your first need], let your heart revive and live!"

(PSALM 69:32, AMP)

With Joy Comes Life

While we are in the place where the water is to the neck and rising, our very lives are at risk and death seems to be inevitable. But when we seek after God, that death wish is replaced by the life from the Giver of Life. Be encouraged by the Word of God; take heart in its promise. The NKJV describes it this way:

"The humble shall see this and be glad; And you who seek God, your hearts shall live"

(PSALM 69:32, NKJV)

God as the giver of life, having breathed into Adam, provides life and hope to the seeker. Therefore, there is a definite association between God and life. Jesus even goes further by describing Himself as the "Bread of Life."

Where we get it wrong is that we expect that we have the inalienable "right" to life. Society has conditioned us to the right of the individual, but this has occurred at the exclusion of the God-concept of grace, whereby regardless of our position or station in life we have access to the same life-giver and, in our emptiness, we are filled with the Glory of God. Grace is not given to us on our terms but through the sacrifice of the perfect one, on a despicable cross, dying in our place.

"For the LORD hears the cries of his needy ones"

(PSALM 69:33A)

Yes, God does hear our cries.

Who are His needy ones? We are all his needy ones. God hears our cries regardless of what we may think or perceive. Even when God doesn't answer our cries, He has answered. Answers always come in the form of "Yes," "No" and "Not yet." Remember, God is God and we should never regard ourselves more highly than we are in comparison to Him.

Be encouraged that God hears our cries. When the water is to the neck and rising, we are in desperation and are very needy indeed.

"He does not despise his people who are oppressed"

(PSALM 69:33B)

Who are the oppressed? The *Amplified Bible* describes these people as the miserable and wounded ones. Peterson talked of God not walking out on those. His heart is for the oppressed and the wretched. God has a definite heart for those who are captive, those who are bound and those who are helpless. His desire is to see liberty come to the oppressed, the chains loosed on the captive.

Outcomes of that Promise

With the promises of God, distinct benefits result. Those promises are neither hollow nor groundless. The benefits of being a recipient of God's promises are shown in the following verses:

There Is Restoration

"For God will save Jerusalem and rebuild the towns of Judah
His people will live there and settle in their own land"

(PSALM 69:35)

Restoration is an interesting word in terms of human well-being. It speaks to me of rebuilding, of bringing back something back to the original state. There is also an implied sense of peacefulness as order has been brought about. The place of restoration is a place of prospering, steadiness, stability and life. There is also contentment in the place of restoration. The restorative work of God is absolutely perfect in all of its ways. God as the Creator and the great architect of humankind knows the intricacies of the human spirit and, as a result, knows exactly what is required to bring about healing and restoration to it.

In a healing context, restoration incorporates health and well-being but there are also the signs of having lived a particular life. If we use the analogy of the floodwaters, then the residual is the mark as to where the water had risen. It serves as a reminder to us, much like a scar from an injury.

God is a rebuilder of lives. The place we inhabit is rebuilt. The walls that have been broken down are built again. Where there is an attitude of praise restoration results. Your lives become a fresh place where there is a settled life. That is what God does; He brings peace and balance to a life that has been subject to the floods of life.

Where there was once conflict there is now salvation and rebuilding. There is also life and settlement. Looking at this passage for the Psalmist to talk about rebuilding an event or events needs to have occurred that has resulted in devastation and the need to rebuild. The same is true in a spiritual context, as is viewed in the physical. Emotionally we are still in the same place as the floodwaters. The torrent has subsided and ebbed away, and along with this salvation that God offers comes a rebuilding, enabling the ability to live again in that place and to be settled in your own land. We are never removed from our environment. We learn to live within those confines and learn to manage our lives.

It is praise that lifts our spirits out of our despair and sets us above the difficulties of life. We need to determine to acknowledge our pain in order to be able to come to that place of praise, and in that place of praise, it seems that all of creation has joined in and there is that desire for that symphony to join with us in joyful praise to God, for His goodness and for His graciousness that are extended to us.

Your Family Benefits

"The descendants of those who obey him will inherit the land"

(Psalm 69:36a)

150

God provides us with a legacy. With God there are no half measures in His promises. When He promises and what He promises are of benefit and of sheer quality. No expense has been spared.

The result of the work of God does not only provide benefits to you, but in a sense, they are also extended to your family. In personal inner healing, the residual of personal peace is peace with and within your family; in relationships in general. Your family participates in the benefits that are yours through the work of restoration.

God is a God of the generations. His blessings are not only immediate, but exist long past our lives. Descendants does not only apply to our progeny, but to their progeny, and so on and so forth, and it all comes down to one simple word: obedience. God desires our all, our submission, and out of that simple act comes inheritance. The promise of God is not withheld but is lavished upon us.

All of the commandments of God that also have a promise are a promise to the generations. Blessings and curses can be generational. The promise to Abram, later renamed Abraham, was that his descendants would be like the stars of the heavens and the grains of sand. Blessings in God's commandments were for the generations, not on the initial recipient. Blessing was transferable to the next generation. Not only do you benefit from peace and living in your own place but also your descendants, who obey God as well, can participate in that same inheritance.

There Will Be Safety

"And those who love him will live there in safety"

(PSALM 69:36B)

What a joy to know that when God does work in your life you will experience safety. This is such a contrast to David's plight at the beginning of the Psalm. David was in a place of personal peril and feared for his very life. The weight of his circumstances were threatening to overtake him; he was "drowning" with the water to his neck and rising. But here we see that the revelation of God reveals that when God hears us and works, He brings us to a place of safety. What a contrast. What joy! To know that God is in control even though we would not be prepared to admit that, and to surrender control to Him can be extremely difficult.

The challenge for each of us who are in the waters up to our necks and rising is to begin to appropriate those things that reveal the goodness of God. That same peace and joy are also for your descendants. It is refreshing to know that he who has begun in a place of peril and utter jeopardy will have descendants is a promise of life. God cares for us in such a way as He will not let us become overcome by the floodwaters, and He gives us safety and sanctuary. But we only come into that place through praise of our Saviour and King.

SUMMARY

The following table is a simple graphic that shows the feelings, emotions, thoughts and attitudes that typify a person experiencing the waters to the neck and rising. There is also an accompanying phrase/statement.

Feelings	
Overwhelmed	"This is too hard."
Exhaustion	"I feel so tired."
Emotions	
Weeping	"I just want to cry."
Anger	"It couldn't have happened to a nicer person."
Thoughts	
God has forgotten me.	"God isn't interested in me." "I have no one, I am all alone."
Broken-hearted	"I feel as though I have been left all alone; no one wants me."
Ridiculed	"Why are you picking on me?"
Alienated	"I feel so alone."

Crying out for deliverance	"I want it to stop."
Loss of trust*	"Who can I trust? There is no one."
Humiliated	"How could they treat me that way?"
Attitudes	
Retribution	"It couldn't have happened to a nicer person."
Loss of trust*	"Who can I trust? There is no one."
Unforgiveness	"I will not forgive you for what you did."
Vengeful	"I hope that bad things happen to you."

Loss of trust can be described as both a thought and an attitude.

Each of these contribute to the state that clinicians call depression. To the person experiencing depression, these thoughts, feelings and emotions are real. Regardless if they are real or a perception of reality, they need to be validated before a sufferer can come through to recovery.

BIBLIOGRAPHY

Barnes. *Notes of the Bible* (1834).

Calvin, John. "Calvin's Commentaries," Christian Classics Ethereal Library.

Clarke, Adam. *Adam Clarke's Commentary on the Bible* (1831).

Cobbet, Thomas.

Darby, John Nelson. "Bible Synopsis" (1857–62).

Deakin University Student Life Feeling Overwhelmed (2007).

Jamieson, Robert, David Brown and Robert Faussett. *A Commentary, Critical, Practical and Explanatory, On the Old and New Testament* (1882).

Gill, John. "Expository of Psalm 69" (1746–63).

Harris and Thoresen. *The Handbook of Unforgiveness.* Chapter 19: Forgiveness, Unforgiveness, Health, and Disease.

Healey. *Anxiety and Depression.*

Henry, Matthew. *Matthew Henry's Commentary on the Whole Bible* (1706).

Jakes, TD. *Loose That Man and Let Him Go* (2000). Inspirational Press, New York.

Keil, Carl Friedrich and Franz Delitzsch. *Biblical Commentary on the Old Testament* (1857–78).

Kidner, Derek. *Old Testament Commentary – Psalms 1–72*. IVP.

Myer. *Man to Man Manual* (2005). Careforce Ministries Limited.

Myers, David G. *Exploring Psychology* (2008). Worth Publishers, New York.

Myers, David G. *The Pursuit of Happiness*. Avon Books.

"Scofield Reference Notes" (*Bible Hub*).

Scott, Elizabeth, M.S. *Journal of Behavioral Medicine*.

Spurgeon, Charles. *Lectures to My Students – Lecture 11*.

Thayer, J. H. *The New Thayer's Greek-English Lexicon* (1981). Hendrickson Publishers, Peabody, Massachusetts.

The ArtsScroll Tanach Series: Tehillim – Psalms. (2002). Mesorah Publications, Ltd., Brooklyn, New York.

"Treasury of Scripture Notes" (*Bible Hub*).

"Wesley Notes" (*Bible Hub*).

Zlotowitz, Rabbi Meir. *The Book of Ruth: Megillas Ruth* (1976). Mesorah Publications, Ltd., New York City.

Websites

Beyond Blue: www.beyondblue.org.au

Biblehub.com: www.biblehub.com

Black Dog Institute: www.blackdog.org.au

Harvard Health: www.health.harvard.edu

Depression and mental illness are said to be the major health issues of the twenty-first century. It is a hidden ailment where, if you observe an individual outwardly, they will look like the next person and our automatic response would be that there is nothing wrong with them. But this is where we make our greatest mistake. We judge based upon our prejudices. It is this judging that results in feelings of alienation and distrust.

We, as a society, need to embrace those who are the sufferers. To learn to understand their plight, help them to feel validated, move forward, begin to function again and provide a valuable contribution. Those who have been able to journey forward and move out of the fog begin to have a different perspective on life.

This book explores the issue of depression from a different position. The emotions, attitudes and thoughts of those sufferers have been developed through observations of Psalm 69 penned by King David.

9 781400 325313